SECOND EDITION
SOCIOLOGY THROUGH ACTIVE LEARNING

SECOND EDITION

SOCIOLOGY THROUGH ACTIVE LEARNING

Student Exercises

Editors

Kathleen McKinney & Barbara S. Heyl

Illinois State University

PINE FORGE PRESS
An Imprint of SAGE Publications, Inc.
Los Angeles • London • New Delhi • Singapore

For information:

Pine Forge Press
A SAGE Publications Company
2455 Teller Road
Thousand Oaks, California 91320
E-mail: order@sagepub.com

SAGE Publications Ltd.
1 Oliver's Yard
55 City Road
London EC1Y 1SP
United Kingdom

SAGE Publications India Pvt. Ltd.
B 1/I 1 Mohan Cooperative
    Industrial Area
Mathura Road, New Delhi 110 044
India

SAGE Publications Asia-Pacific Pte. Ltd.
33 Pekin Street #02-01
Far East Square
Singapore 048763

Printed in the United States of America.

Library of Congress Cataloging-in-Publication Data

Sociology through active learning: student exercises/editors, Kathleen McKinney, Barbara S. Heyl.—2nd ed.
    p. cm.
Rev. ed. of: Sociology through active learning/Kathleen McKinney. 2001.
ISBN 978-1-4129-5703-8 (pbk.)
    1. Sociology—Problems, exercises, etc. 2. Active learning—Problems, exercises, etc. I. McKinney, Kathleen.
II. Heyl, Barbara Sherman, III. McKinney, Kathleen. Sociology through active learning.

HM575.M39 2009
301.076—dc22   2008011801

This book is printed on acid-free paper.

11   12   10   9   8   7   6   5   4   3   2

Acquisitions Editor:	Benjamin Penner
Editorial Assistant:	Nancy Scrofano
Production Editor:	Karen Wiley
Copy Editor:	Monica Burden
Proofreader:	Kristen Bergstad
Typesetter:	C&M Digitals (P) Ltd.
Cover Designer:	Candice Harman
Marketing Manager:	Jennifer Reed Banando

Contents

A Note From the Editors to the Students   xiii

1   THEORY AND METHODS   1

Puzzling Over Theoretical Perspectives   3
Kathleen Lowney, Valdosta State University

Are you nervous about theory? This exercise is a fun way to begin to think about the role of theory in the discipline of sociology. You will be asked to get into a group and then collectively work a puzzle under timed conditions. This task can help reduce any anxiety that you might have about working with theories.

The Speed Discussion   7
Peter Kaufman, State University of New York at New Paltz

Although most of us are comfortable engaging in informal chitchat with each other, talking about social theory is a bona fide conversation killer. But it doesn't have to be this way. This exercise will get us talking to each other about social theory in much the same way that we talk to each other about less academic subjects. After completing this exercise you will have a better understanding of how social theory relates to your life and the lives of your classmates.

Faculty Doors as Symbolic Statements   11
John W. Eby, Messiah College

This active exercise uses naturally occurring symbolic statements—postings on faculty office doors—to help you develop skills of observation, understand the sociological imagination, develop group cohesion, and understand one aspect of campus culture. What do your faculty members post on their doors?

A Very Short Survey   15
Susan M. Collins, University of Northern Colorado, and Sue R. Crull, Iowa State University

Here is your chance to choose a research topic with your classmates, to operationalize that concept, to write survey questions that get at the issue, to collect the data, and to interpret that information. Welcome to sociology.

Helping Experiment   19
Paul Higgins, University of South Carolina at Columbia, and Mitchell B. Mackinem, Claflin University

You will experience and explore the challenge of creating knowledge about social life through an important research method used by sociologists: experiments. You will also work with the scientific process, the steps through which sociologists and other scientists conduct their investigations. This experiment explores whether attachment between people affects whether help is offered.

An Introduction to an Important Source for Basic Quantitative Sociological Data 23
Edward L. Kain, Southwestern University

A central component of sociology is asking sociological questions and exploring them with data. One of the first steps in this process involves learning about sources of sociological data. This exercise introduces you to one such source, the website for the U.S. Census Bureau, and helps you to begin to think about how social variables can be measured.

2 CULTURE 27

Decoding Human Behavior: Social Norms and Daily Life 29
Corinne Lally Benedetto, DePaul University

Every social situation functions through the recognition and maintenance of norms. These prescriptions for appearance and behavior are both formal (written) and informal (expected), yet we typically pay little conscious attention to them. This assignment (group and individual) offers systematic practice in the recognition and analysis of norms in everyday life situations.

Understanding Social Location 45
Andrea Malkin Brenner, American University

By reading and discussing some shocking fictional accounts, we hope you will come to see that as humans, we have a habit of looking at other people's worlds as we look into our own. We make assumptions based on what we know is the norm or believe to be the truth. But others in a different social location might see things differently.

Application Exercise on Ethnocentrism and Cultural Relativism 51
Virginia Teas Gill, Illinois State University

In this group writing assignment, you will learn to view the world with different lenses by analyzing specific cases or situations. The focus is on the concepts of ethnocentrism and cultural relativism. How do people from different cultures view an event, and why might they view the same event differently?

Peer Learning in Sociology: Learning About Other Cultures From International Students 55
Beth Pamela Skott, University of Bridgeport

So many times we read about abstract concepts in sociology textbooks and then just move on. This exercise allows you to take some of these concepts further. Through conversations and interactions with international students, you will get the chance to learn more about other cultures and understand some of the abstract sociological concepts. This is also an excellent opportunity to practice applying sociological concepts to other societies.

Observing Culture 63
Craig This, Sinclair Community College

Do eating establishments have a culture? What are the values, norms, mores, folkways, languages, symbols, and technology used in that culture? In this assignment, you will do a direct observation of an eating establishment to answer these questions.

3 SOCIALIZATION, INTERACTION, AND GROUP INFLUENCE 67

Writing Children's Books 69
Peter Kaufman, State University of New York at New Paltz

Do you remember some of your favorite children's books? Have you ever stopped to consider the content and the messages of these books? This exercise will get us thinking more sociologically about children's literature so that we can better understand the ways in which these books contribute to our socialization.

Gender Socialization 73

Betsy Lucal, Indiana University at South Bend

The purpose of this individual and group exercise is to give you a chance to analyze how children learn about gender. You will begin with a visit to a children's clothing or toy store so that you can observe the items that are offered for sale. By analyzing the gender makeup of children's toys and/or clothes, you will have a chance to see how gender and socialization work in the real world.

Leadership, Gender, and the Invisible Ceiling: Survey Activity 77

Keith A. Roberts, Hanover College

This activity is a survey exercise in which you gather some data from about 25 students—male and female—that enable us to reflect on social conceptions of masculinity and femininity and our society's definitions of leadership. Understanding that our definitions of leadership characteristics tend to correspond very highly to our society's definitions of masculinity can help us understand forces that contribute to the invisible ceiling.

NASA: Understanding Social Interaction 85

Heather M. Griffiths, Fayetteville State University

This exercise, based on a popular NASA problem-solving exercise, is ideal for introducing you to important concepts related to the study of society and social interaction. It is a great way to transition into specialized vocabulary (i.e., proxemic communication, kinesic communication, paralinguistic communication). This versatile exercise is also useful as an icebreaker, introducing you and your peers to issues of race, gender, and the sociological imagination.

Group Decision Making 91

Judy L. Singleton, College of Mount St. Joseph

Building on previous group assignments, this exercise enables you to analyze what factors about your group influenced how the process worked. What might explain the particular dynamics of your group? Did leaders or other roles emerge? Can you track how decisions were made? Learning to analyze group dynamics can be a valuable skill to take into your future workplace.

4 STRATIFICATION 97

Six Statements for Teaching Social Stratification 99

Lissa J. Yogan, Valparaiso University

Do you wonder why some see the United States as the land of opportunity and others do not? This activity will ask you to work individually and in groups to examine common beliefs about an individual's opportunity to get ahead. By the end of the discussion you will be able to relate ascribed statuses to people's acceptance or rejection of the idea that everyone has the opportunity to "get ahead" in the United States.

Guided Fantasy: The *Titanic* Game 105

John R. Bowman, University of North Carolina at Pembroke

This time, your ship is going down, survivors will be few, and your group will have to make life-and-death decisions. This exercise will bring issues of social status and social inequality into focus, as was the case with the real Titanic and the list of who actually survived its sinking. Do you think that social class position still affects life-and-death decisions?

Food Stamp Challenge 109

Sandra Enos, Bryant University

For many of us without direct experience with welfare and family support programs, we assume that our welfare programs provide enough support for needy families who are dependent on state aid and we also imagine that getting this help is relatively easy. This exercise is designed to introduce you to the challenges of living on a food stamp budget. You will review a typical application for food stamp benefits, plan out a week's menu, and consider the challenges of living within this budget and what you would do if your food planning ran short.

Making Ends Meet — 113
Mellisa Holtzman, Ball State University

Have you ever wondered how much a middle-class lifestyle costs? This exercise will help you estimate the income needed by a family of four in order to support a middle-class lifestyle. Then it will ask you to compare those figures to the income levels of a family in poverty and to think about the goods and services that family must do without in order to "make ends meet" on their income.

Global Inequality: Comparing Guinea to the United States — 117
Fadia Joseph and Donal J. Malone, Saint Peter's College

Does the country in which we live influence our chances in life? This assignment is designed to help you understand global inequality and its impact on the life chances of people living in developed and less developed countries. In the process, we explore the sociological perspective and how it illustrates how our lives are shaped by the society in which we are raised.

Global Stratification and Its Impact on a Country's Population Characteristics — 125
Edward L. Kain, Southwestern University

Population statistics can provide a very useful tool for understanding variation between countries, including the impact of global stratification on basic life chances. In this exercise you will choose two countries at different places in the global system of stratification—a wealthy country and a poorer country. Once you have chosen these countries you will compare and contrast them in terms of basic population characteristics.

5 ORGANIZATIONS, BUREAUCRACY, AND WORK/OCCUPATIONS — 129

Team Case Study of a Community Organization — 131
Rebecca Bach, Duke University

Are you feeling thoroughly depressed after examining so many serious social issues? In this project you will have the opportunity to begin to envision potential solutions to social problems. You will study a local community organization that is working to ameliorate poverty, crime, drug abuse, teen pregnancy, environmental degradation, and more. How effective is the organization? What would you do differently?

Structural Change at Your College or University — 135
Charles S. Green III, University of Wisconsin at Whitewater (Retired)

By comparing a much older organizational chart of your school with one from today, you will be able to see how your college or university has changed structurally as an organization. What kinds of changes have occurred, and what might explain these changes? See whether you can relate these organizational changes to other changes that have occurred both inside and outside your college or university during this time period.

Critique of Student Government — 139
Alton M. Okinaka, University of Hawai'i at Hilo

Here is an opportunity to consider what you would like your student government to do for you and then to investigate systematically what it is currently doing. This government operates right on your doorstep, which makes it accessible to you. Or is it accessible? You will have the chance to work with a group over a number of weeks to find out how closely this government in operation meets your vision.

Occupation and Income Exercise   145
  Keith A. Roberts, Hanover College

  In this exercise, you are asked to consider why we pay more for some jobs than others. Your group will have to divide a specific sum among workers who are doing different kinds of work. On what basis do you decide who gets what amount of income? Sociologists try to explain patterns in society. Do their theories help you analyze and explain the different levels of income associated with different jobs?

Fast Food, Fast Talk: Interactive Service Work   149
  Catherine Fobes and Adam Gillis, Alma College

  Have you ever worked in the fast food industry? As service workers, service recipients, or managers, Interactive Service Work (ISW) impacts us on a daily basis. Using McDonald's is a fun way to help you explore the components and complexities of ISW.

6 RACE AND GENDER   153

Thinking Critically About Race Through Visual Media   155
  Marcia Marx and Mary Thierry Texeira, California State University, San Bernardino

  In a major group project over a number of weeks, you will tape from the television examples of subtle messages about non-white groups. Presenting your edited selections to your whole class will enable you to show and tell how the media can make certain images of different racial groups seem to be a natural part of the way things are in society (when, in fact, they are manipulating that picture).

Drawing Pictures: Race and Gender Stereotypes   163
  Jacqueline C. Simpson, Guilford Technical Community College

  We all have stereotypes in our minds, and this exercise helps get some of them out on the table— literally. Doing this activity early in a course will help you see the ways in which we organize an image of people in our minds and even adapt the names that we give to people to fit that image.

"Stump That Race" Game   169
  Melanie D. Hildebrandt, Indiana University of Pennsylvania

  Most people get really nervous when the subject of race comes up in a class or other mixed race setting. This exercise is a fun and playful way to diffuse that anxiety and begin to learn how a person's race influences what we know—or don't know—about each other.

A Group Exercise in Affirmative Action   173
  Jacqueline C. Simpson, Guilford Technical Community College

  To do this exercise, you will need to apply the Civil Rights Act of 1964 and its executive order to specific situations, such as admitting certain students (and not others) to medical school or, in the case of a private firm, promoting some workers to supervisory positions. You will need to devise a plan to guide and justify your decisions while upholding the law, but you will have your group to help you.

Analyzing the Social Construction of Gender in Birth Announcement Cards   177
  Jacqueline Clark, Ripon College, and Maxine Atkinson, North Carolina State University

  How is gender socially constructed? By analyzing the images and text found in greeting cards for new parents, this exercise helps you to see some of the ways gender is created and reenacted by humans.

Reading *Little Critter*: Understanding the Power of Symbols 181
Jacqueline C. Simpson, Guilford Technical Community College

Relive your childhood and learn about the power of symbols at the same time! This exercise asks you to read Little Critter with a more critical, sociological eye and to understand your assumptions about the sex of Little Critter.

7   CRIME AND DEVIANCE 185

Debating Deviance 187
Brenda L. Beagan, Dalhousie University

This exercise will enable you to explore in depth the key concept of deviance. Answering the worksheet questions requires consulting your book chapter on deviance and then working with your classmates to develop a group answer. Groups will then debate each other as to whether or not date rape can be considered deviant, according to the definitions that you developed. This practice in how to build a coherent, logical argument will help develop an essential skill for your academic work and beyond.

Deviance Mini Case Study 193
Janis McCoy, Itawamba Community College

Sociological theories are not developed in a vacuum—they are the product of observation and intense study. They are real life. By writing examples to illustrate theories of deviance you will make these theories come alive.

Images of Crime 203
Paul Higgins, University of South Carolina at Columbia, and Mitchell Mackinem, Claflin University

You and your classmates will conduct a small interview survey in order to identify the common images that people have about crime and criminals. Pooling the findings from all class members, you can consider what patterns emerge from these respondents. Often, the images that we carry with us oversimplify reality and leave out important categories and characteristics.

Media Portrayals of Crime 207
Rebecca L. Bordt, DePauw University

Most Americans rely on the media to get information about the world around them. Is doing so a good idea? This group assignment allows you to test the accuracy of media portrayals of crime in this country by analyzing the content of a major newspaper. Based on your findings, you should be able to say whether it is wise for us to use the New York Times as a primary source for our understanding of crime.

Drug Testing in the Workplace: What Would You Do? 211
Robert B. Pettit, Manchester College

In a hypothetical case study, the owner of an accounting firm begins conducting mandatory drug testing of employees, and one male employee (single, age 28) tests positive. He denies illegal drug use. You and your group need to decide what should happen next. The exercise enables you to debate the real-life issue of mandatory drug testing in the workplace as well as analyze what sociological theories say about how people get identified as deviant and with what consequences.

8   SOCIAL INSTITUTIONS 215

Housework: Division of Labor 217
Judy Aulette, University of North Carolina at Charlotte

This assignment gets you thinking personally about what a couple should do (if anything) to change how household labor is divided between two working parents. You will also place your thoughts in the context of a theoretical approach within sociology.

Parenthood: Defining Family 221
Judy Aulette, University of North Carolina at Charlotte

In order to confront changing definitions of what constitutes a family, you will be asked to decide by whom Baby M, born to a surrogate mother, should be raised. What are the sociological issues relevant to this decision?

Family History Project 225
Mark R. Warren, Harvard University

With this exercise, you have the opportunity to explore in depth your own family history. You will conduct interviews with six family members, going back as many generations as possible. As you and your classmates share stories, you will see the impact of common social and historical factors as well as individual differences. Your final essay will consider both the extent of societal influences on your family and the influence of that family history on who you are today.

Tommy's Story 229
Marjorie Altergott, DePaul University

Define health. This exercise will have you read a case study and then consider definitions of health and other tough questions related to why some people die and others do not. Good luck—this activity involves difficult choices.

Mapping Census Data for Your Town 233
Julie A. Pelton, Illinois Wesleyan University, and Frank D. Beck, Illinois State University

You are asked to look at the poverty rates, racial diversity, and housing characteristics for your hometown or neighborhood. Given what you know of the place, you are asked to describe why these structural characteristics are distributed the way they are. Where do the wealthy live, and why? How segregated are different neighborhoods, and why? Answer these questions and more with Internet mapping technologies.

9 MULTI-TOPIC EXERCISES 241

Song Analysis Project 243
Mellisa Holtzman, Ball State University

Music is sociology? It can be, and this assignment enables you to use the content of different songs as examples of sociological concepts. You might even get a chance to bring compact discs of your own into class to demonstrate the sociological relevance of that music.

"All of a Sudden. . .:" Exploring Sociology in Everyday Life 247
Sarah E. Rusche and Kris Macomber, North Carolina State University

Sociology is all around you—you just have to know what to look for. This active learning assignment requires you to pay closer attention to the social world around you. Through observing your everyday life and the situations and interactions that comprise it, you will see how your social realities are both unique and patterned in important ways. This activity will help you cultivate your sociological imagination.

Critical Reports on Contemporary Social Problems 255
John J. Shalanski, Luzerne County Community College

You will choose a social problem in your local community, in the nation, or a more global issue that affects everyone. Writing critically about the problem that you select, and attempting to come up with solutions, will help you clarify your own perspective and values. You will be able to look at how the problem originated, what has been written about it, and what can be done about it.

Literary and Artistic Reflections on War, Terror, and Violence   259
Danielle Taana Smith, Rochester Institute of Technology

How do we begin to make sense of seemingly senseless acts of war and terror around the world, and violence both globally and within our local communities? We are shocked and overwhelmed with feelings of fear and helplessness as we witness escalations of violence globally, nationally, and locally. This assignment provides a forum for you to examine underlying causes and consequences of violence; to express your reflections through art, poetry, and creative and critical essays; and to share your expressions with a wider audience through postings on a website.

10 COURSE STRUCTURE AND PROCESS   265

Student Empowerment: Student-Designed Syllabus   267
Ada Haynes, Tennessee Technological University

In this group exercise, you will have the opportunity to help design the syllabus for a sociology course. According to the research, such input can increase your motivation, empowerment, and real-world problem-solving skills.

MyPage: Student Information   271
Janis McCoy, Itawamba Community College

What would you like for your instructor to know about you? This assignment will give you the opportunity to creatively introduce yourself.

Initial Group Assessment   277
John R. Bowman, University of North Carolina at Pembroke

Working in groups, you will engage in an analysis of how a class work group (for a class project or assignment) is functioning. You will look at group norms and periodically assess the effectiveness of your group.

Panel Debates   283
Kathleen R. Johnson, Keene State College

Given that there are some controversial yet sociological issues that your class will not have time to address fully, this exercise enables groups to work together to form an argument on one such topic. Different groups in class will argue the pro and con sides of an issue. In doing so, you will become more skilled at constructing quality arguments for what you believe.

About the Editors   289

Note From the Editors to the Students

Your instructor has selected this book for your use to help you learn sociology through active engagement. He or she will have access to an instructor CD that will provide him or her with additional information and materials necessary to help you with these exercises.

We designed the book of active learning exercises with you and your learning in mind. We selected exercises that will help you learn important sociological ideas and allow you to practice your sociological imagination. Research shows that anytime we actually get to do something, we understand it better. An old Chinese proverb puts it this way:

"I hear, and I forget.

"I see, and I remember.

"I do, and I understand."

The book will help your instructor to make use of Chickering and Gamson's "Seven Principles for Good Practice in Undergraduate Education" (http://honolulu.hawaii.edu/intranet/committees/FacDevCom/guidebk/teachtip/7princip.htm). These teaching–learning principles are associated with improved learning and include the following:

1. encourages contact between students and faculty,

2. develops reciprocity and cooperation among students,

3. encourages active learning,

4. gives prompt feedback,

5. emphasizes time on task,

6. communicates high expectations, and

7. respects diverse talents and ways of learning.

You will gain another benefit of doing things and exploring, in that during the process you uncover new things and become engaged with what you are learning. Sociology has a long history of uncovering patterns in the social world of which most people are not aware because they are embedded in the patterns. These exercises will help you "see" the patterns and social processes. We fully expect that these activities will not only help you to do well in your sociology classes, but also open you up to new ways of seeing the social world.

These exercises were developed by real faculty members and used successfully in teaching students similar to you all over the nation. As you look over the exercises in the student book, you will see that all the authors of the exercises have written rationales for their assignments that include what learning goals they had in mind when devising their projects. Next come instructions to you about how to complete the exercise. Finally, each exercise has one or more tear-out worksheets for you to complete and submit to your instructor. Your instructor will explain which exercises to do, when, how, and any grading criteria. These authors have all used these exercises in their own classes and know what student learning is fostered by the process of doing these activities.

We have selected a variety of types of assignments: some can be done individually, some in small groups, some will take place over many weeks, and some can be done during class time. Although most of the exercises are designed to further your substantive understanding of sociological content, we have included a set of exercises at the end of the book dedicated to issues of process in your class.

We wish you well in these explorations of sociology through active learning. We dedicate this workbook to all students—past, present, and future—developing a sociological imagination.

Kathleen McKinney
Barbara S. Heyl

1 Theory and Methods

Puzzling Over Theoretical Perspectives

Kathleen Lowney, Valdosta State University

Rationale

This exercise is a fun way to begin to think about the role of theory in the discipline of sociology. You will be asked to get into a group and then collectively work a puzzle, under timed conditions.

Instructions

1. Your instructor will guide you into forming groups. Most likely, your group will want to get on the floor, so create some floor space for yourselves.

2. Your group will receive a sealed envelope. In it will be puzzle pieces. Do not open the envelope until your professor says to begin. Your group's goal is to work as much of the puzzle as possible in the amount of time given.

3. You will need to both participate in working the puzzle **and**, at the same time, take mental notes on the processes your group uses to solve the puzzle. Eventually, you will need to write down these mental notes, so watch carefully.

4. After time is called, you will be given additional information about your group's puzzle. Then you will be given more time to complete the puzzle. Again, both participate and also observe the group processes. Then you will be given still more information with which to work the puzzle. Can your group get it completely put together this time?

5. Have some fun!

6. Class discussion will require you to think about how certain kinds of puzzle pieces function in ways similar to theories in sociology. Pay close attention to this; you will be asked to explain this in a short essay on the worksheet!

Grading

1. Students must thoroughly answer all questions on the worksheet. Your answers must show a good-faith effort to complete each section of the worksheet.

2. The worksheet must be turned in by the beginning of the next class session.

3. Grading will be explained by your professor in class.

Puzzling Over Theoretical Perspectives

Worksheet

Name: _____

PART I: Write down your observations about how your group worked the puzzles. Think about what kinds of strategies were suggested by group members, which strategies were actually followed, how successful the strategies were, what you learned about the functions of various kind of pieces, and so on.

    A. When the group was given only the first envelope with puzzle pieces:
        Strategies that group members suggested?

        Strategies you actually followed?

        Success of the strategies followed?

        What you learned about the functions of the various kinds of pieces (etc.)?

    B. When the group received the first kind of additional information:
        Strategies that group members suggested?

        Strategies you actually followed?

Success of the strategies followed?

What you learned about the functions of the various kinds of pieces (etc.)?

C. When the group had received all the information needed to work the puzzle:
    Strategies that group members suggested?

Strategies you actually followed?

Success of the strategies followed?

What you learned about the functions of the various kinds of pieces (etc.)?

PART II: Please write in the space below what you learned about the role of theory in sociology from doing this exercise. Think about the role of border pieces, the interior pieces, how information such as the picture helped you to understand what the puzzle was about. What are the comparable analogies in sociological theory? Explain. Discuss how this analogy between sociological theory and the border pieces of puzzles can help you as you study a particular set of data.

The Speed Discussion

Peter Kaufman, State University of
New York at New Paltz

Rationale

It has been noted that we can learn more if we discuss things with others. Listening to just one voice in class (usually the instructor's) does not maximize our learning potential. Instead, we should strive to hear as many viewpoints as possible. Even if some people do not fully comprehend the material, hearing them articulate their confusion may help us (as well as them). This is particularly true in trying to decipher sociological theory. Many students are confused and turned off by the writings of classical sociological theorists. Not only do these older theorists often use an antiquated linguistic style but their arguments are complex, wordy, and rely on historical references that most students know little about. And yet, we still read classical theory in sociology because it helps us understand the social world we live in today. The challenge for teachers and learners is to decode these sociological theories and figure out how they are relevant to our everyday lives. The Speed Discussion was created to do just that. By fostering dialogue with an array of people, and by having students share with each other the various ways in which sociological theory relates to their everyday lives, the Speed Discussion will help the class develop a collective understanding of some key sociological theorists.

Instructions

Each member of the class will write a few sentences about some questions and then we will discuss our answers with each other in groups of two. Each group will discuss their answers for only three minutes, and then we will change partners and discuss the same question again with another partner. Once we have discussed each question with three people, we will move to the next question. We will continue in this fashion until we have discussed all of the questions with three different people. *Please make sure that you introduce yourself to the other person.*

Grading

See your instructor for details concerning how this assignment will be graded.

The Speed Discussion

Worksheet

Name: _____

Take a few minutes to write down some thoughts to the following questions:

1. Karl Marx: In one of his famous quotes Marx said, "The ideas of the ruling class are the ruling ideas." Think about whether you agree or disagree with Marx and come up with an example or two to support your argument.

2. Max Weber: Think of some situations where you obey authority. In these instances, do you obey this authority because of rational authority (formal rules), traditional authority (established beliefs), or charismatic authority (personal qualities of the leader)? Are there any instances where you obey authority for some other reason?

3. W. E. B. DuBois: In one of the first sociological analyses on race, DuBois made the following statement: "The problem of the twentieth century is the problem of the color-line—the relation of the darker to the lighter races of men in Asia and Africa, in America and the islands of the sea." Do you think this statement is still accurate today? In other words, is the problem of the twenty-first century still the problem of the color line?

Faculty Doors As Symbolic Statements

John W. Eby, Messiah College

Rationale

This active exercise uses naturally occurring symbolic statements—postings on office doors—to help you develop skills of observation, understand the sociological imagination, develop group cohesion, and understand one aspect of campus culture. Postings on faculty doors are symbolic statements of individuals and symbolic representations of the subcultures in the area in which the doors are located.

Instructions

Your class will be formed into groups and assigned to visit various campus buildings or sections of buildings in order to "read" the subculture of the area by observing what is posted on office doors. Record your observations on the worksheet and on other pages as necessary.

You should be prepared to explain what you are doing to anyone who asks. You should also talk with those people who are in the offices that you examine. If time allows, your instructor might ask you to interview the person in the office. Remember that what people post on their doors is affected by many things. Many of these are personal. Others are structural, such as rules that limit what people may post.

Grading

See your instructor for details regarding how this exercise will be graded.

Faculty Doors As Symbolic Statements

Worksheet

Names of group members:

Area observed:

Postings on office doors are symbolic statements that tell a lot about the person (or persons) in the offices, about the subculture of the area where the office is located, and about institutional rules about postings. Examine the doors in the area assigned by your instructor. Carefully observe and record below what is posted on the doors and the areas surrounding the doors. Note both style and content. Look for the "what," and deduce the "why." Think comparatively. How is your area different from other areas on campus?

Use the space below, and extra sheets if needed, to do the following things:

1. List what is on the doors. Develop general categories (e.g., cartoons, course-related announcements, profound sayings, things related to family).

2. Comment on the style of the postings (are they neat, messy, etc.).

3. Make deductions from what you observe about what the faculty member does and what personal characteristics the faculty member might have. Also make deductions about the subculture of the area in which the office is located.

4. Identify variables that might explain what you observe, and suggest hypotheses based on these variables.

5. Evaluate this methodology. What other methodologies could be used to gather data and to test your hypotheses?

A Very Short Survey

Susan M. Collins, University of Northern Colorado, and Sue R. Crull, Iowa State University

Rationale

The goal for the "very short survey" is for you to join with other students to develop three survey questions during one class period. Through this brief process you will learn some basics about writing survey questions. Also, with your individual report following the analysis of the data, you will learn some basics about interpretation of data analysis that will help you to better understand the topic you chose to study.

Instructions

1. During the first five minutes of class, you and other students will choose a survey topic.

2. Then for about 10–15 minutes you will break into small discussion groups to operationalize the topic by developing three closed-ended questions, including response categories. One student from your group then writes the questions on the chalk board.

3. Finally, the whole class comes back together to evaluate and edit the questions, and choose the three they want on the survey. You can combine or eliminate similar questions, refine the wording, and adjust response categories. Then you will vote by a show of hands for the final three questions.

4. Your instructor will explain how the data will be collected and analyzed.

5. Following the analysis of the data, you will review a cross tabulation of two variables from the survey and write a brief summary interpreting the results of the survey analysis.

Grading

Your interpretative summary will likely be evaluated on content accuracy, organization, and presentation. Please see your instructor for details on grading.

A Very Short Survey

Worksheet: Interpretative Summary

Name: _____

Please provide your cross-tabulation table below:

Write a brief summary interpreting the cross-tabulation results.

Helping Experiment

Paul Higgins, University of South Carolina
at Columbia, and Mitchell B. Mackinem,
Claflin University

Rationale

You will experience and explore the challenge of creating knowledge about social life through an important research method used by sociologists: experiments. You can also work with the scientific process, the steps through which sociologists and other scientists conduct their investigations. This experiment explores whether attachments between people affect whether help is offered. Two people are attached when they like each other or when they have affection for each other. Sociologists consider attachments crucial for social life and have explored their importance in many areas of social behavior, such as conversion to religious groups and deviant behavior.

Instructions

Your instructor may modify these instructions. Check with your instructor.

1. Decide on some objects to be dropped, such as books, notebooks, coins, or whatever. Several or more items should be dropped.

2. Drop the objects in front of a stranger as the stranger passes by. Do so in a way that appears natural.

3. Record whether the stranger helps you pick up the dropped items.

4. Drop the same objects in front of a friend. Do so in a way that appears natural.

5. Record whether your friend helps you pick up the dropped items.

6. Bring your results to class to be combined with the results from your classmates.

7. With the results from your classmates, create a two-by-two table (see worksheet). This activity can be done in class with your professor. The causal dimension, (degree of) attachment (to a passerby), can be classified into two conditions: friend and stranger. The outcome dimension, helping, can be classified as yes or no.

8. Fill in each cell of the table with the appropriate results from your and your classmates' experimental trials.

9. Calculate the percentage of strangers who helped and did not help and the percentage of friends who helped and did not help.

10. Examine and interpret your results.

Grading Criteria

Check with your instructor. Grading criteria can include how clearly you present your conclusions, whether you show how the results support your conclusions, and your careful discussion of how the conduct of the experiment might have affected the results and how the experiment could be conducted more adequately.

Helping Experiment

Worksheet

Name: _____

| | Attachment | |
| Friend | | Stranger |

Yes _____

Helped

No _____

100 percent   100 percent

1. Examine your results. Were friends more or less likely to help than strangers?

2. What conclusions do you draw about the importance of attachments for helping? Discuss how the results support your conclusions.

3. Evaluate how you and your classmates conducted the experiment. Discuss how the conduct of the experiment could be improved.

An Introduction to an Important Source for Basic Quantitative Data

Edward L. Kain, Southwestern University

Rationale

Sociological analysis involves both theory and research. Sociologists use theory to develop hypotheses about how different variables are empirically related in the social world. An important first step in developing your sociological imagination is learning about key sources of data that can be used to explore sociological questions. This assignment introduces you to one important source of sociological data, the website of the United States Census Bureau.

This assignment has three simple goals–to introduce you to one source of data that you might find useful in sociology and other classes, to have you start to think about variation in several social variables, and to help you think a bit about how we might measure social variables.

Instructions

The instructions are included on the worksheet below. As noted on the worksheet, you need to:

1. Choose two different counties or cities.

2. Print the data for: (a) the two cities/counties you have chosen, (b) the state or states in which those cities/counties are located, and (c) the entire United States.

3. Be prepared to discuss the data in class on the day the assignment is due.

4. Make certain you are prepared to discuss the measurement of the variables, with a particular focus upon the measures of race/ethnicity.

5. Write out your answers to the questions in Part VI on the worksheet.

6. Because we will discuss this assignment in class, it is important that you bring it with you to class. To receive full credit you must have it completed and with you at the beginning of class on the day it is due.

Grading

See your instructor for information about grading this exercise in your course.

An Introduction to an Important Source for Basic Quantitative Data

Worksheet

Name: _____

For this assignment:

1. Go to the following Web address at the U.S. Census Bureau Website: http://quickfacts.census.gov/qfd

2. Choose two different counties or two different cities. You can choose both of them from your home state, or you can compare a county or city from one state with that in another state. It would be ideal to have a range of states and counties/cities, so in class we'll talk about what states and counties/cities you plan to choose. It would be great if you'd look at your home county/city as well as one that interests you in another state.

   For the two counties or two cities you chose for this exercise:

3. Print the data for the state (or states) that you have chosen. (This will list a set of variables for the state as well as the entire U.S.) Also print out the data for the two counties/cities you have chosen. This sheet will list data on a variety of variables for the county/city, as well as for the state in which the county or city is found.

4. Look through the data, and be ready to discuss them in class.

5. Choose one of the race variables (% Asian persons, % African American persons, etc.). Be sure that you know how this was measured.

   Race variable that you chose:

   How was it measured?

   Choose another variable of your choice and read about how that variable was measured.

   Name of the other variable you chose:

   How was it measured?

6. Briefly (a couple of sentences for each question is fine) answer each of the questions below.
   A. What percentage of your two counties/cities is composed of persons 65 years old and over?

   How does this compare to the percentage in the entire state(s) that are the same age?

   How does it compare to the percentage in the United States as a whole?

   B. What is the average number of persons per household in each of the two counties/cities that you chose?

   How does this compare to the state(s) and the whole country?

   C. What is the percentage of people below poverty in the two counties/cities?

   In the state(s)?

   In the United States?

   D. Of all of the variables, which one or two surprised you the most?

   Why?

On the day this is due in class, you will hand in both the printed data sheets and your answers to these questions. Please have them stapled together (or at least make certain your name is on all sheets). As noted in the instructions, you need to be prepared to talk about these data in class.

2   Culture

Decoding Human Behavior

Social Norms and Daily Life

Corinne Lally Benedetto, DePaul University

Rationale

In this set of three exercises, you will investigate the connection between human behavior and the organization of daily social experience. People's interactions with each other take place in social environments that can be studied and observed. Studying social environments helps us to understand the ways people engage with each other and the meaning of human behavior. For instance, a typical school classroom conveys numerous written (formal) and unwritten (informal) expectations for human behavior. Social scientists refer to these expectations as *norms*. Norms guide people's actions, appearance, and even internal perspective; decoding them helps us retain control and individual responsibility for the things we do. People often accept the guidance of social norms, but there are times when we reject their shaping function in social life. Social scientists are extremely interested in this phenomenon, and call it *social deviance*. Any systematic observation of a social environment will produce evidence of both kinds of responses. As students of social life, we are most interested in interpreting the reasons for these responsive human behaviors.

Some specific learning objectives for the several exercises in this assignment are as follows:

- Practice Exercises 1 and 2: Identifying at least five formal and informal norms in a common social environment during two different observation periods.
- Field Studies I and II: Analyzing the connection of social norms to the physical environment.
- Interpreting the shaping effect of social norms on human behavior.

Instructions

Instructions for the separate exercises precede the corresponding worksheet(s).

Grading

Grading and assessment of these three exercises will take into account the level of intellectual engagement shown by the finished exercise worksheets. Criteria used by individual instructors in assessing observational exercises can vary; however, they are likely to include credit for clearly articulated observations and well-reasoned interpretation of data and their meaning.

Decoding Human Behavior: Social Norms and Daily Life

Instructions for First and Second Practice Exercises

Each of you will choose one social environment to study. This should be a common social environment; easily accessible and open to public observation. During two thirty-minute periods, you will make observations of basic social norms and their functions. You will present aspects of the field observations to your classmates for question and critique.

Required steps to follow:

1. Identify the social environment you will observe and the two periods of time you plan to be there. Record this information on the first and second "Practice Observation Worksheets."

2. Bring your student identification card and a notebook to record your observations every time you enter the field.

3. Be attentive to the way the social environment is physically organized, as well as its emotional tone or feeling.

Instructions for Field Study I

Each of you will choose one social environment to study. This should be (1) a *familiar* social context, and (2) different from the practice environment. Please choose a common social environment, one that is open to public observation. During one sixty-minute period, you will make observations of social norms, arrangement of social space, and various human behaviors. You will present aspects of the field observations to classmates for observation and critique, as well as a written analysis for assessment and grading.

Required steps to follow:

1. Identify the social environment you will observe, and the date and time you will be in the field. Record this information on the "Field Study I Worksheet."

2. Bring your student identification card and a notebook to record your observations every time you enter the field.

3. Be attentive to the physical organization of the environment, its emotional tone and feeling, and the various human behaviors that occur within it. Record this information on the "Field Study I Worksheet."

4. Use your notes from the field observation to write a three-page analysis of the way social norms and human behavior appear to be connected in this environment.

Instructions for Field Study II

Each of you will choose one social environment to study. This should be (1) an *unfamiliar* social context, and (2) different from the Practice and Field Study I environments. Please choose a common social environment, one that is open to public observation. During one sixty-minute period, you will make observations of social norms, arrangement of social space, and various human behaviors. You will present aspects of the field observations to classmates for observation and critique, as well as a written analysis for assessment and grading.

Required steps to follow:

1. Identify the social environment you will observe, and the date and time you will be in the field. Record this information on the "Field Study II Worksheet."

2. Bring your student identification card and a notebook to record your observations every time you enter the field.

3. Be attentive to the physical organization of the environment, its emotional tone and feeling, and the various human behaviors that occur within it. Record this information on the "Field Study II Worksheet."

4. Use your notes from the field observation to write a three-page analysis of the way social norms and human behavior appear to be connected in this environment.

Decoding Human Behavior: Social Norms and Daily Life

Worksheet 1: First Practice Observation

Name: _____

1. Description of Social Environment:

2. Date of Second Practice Observation:

3. Time Begun:

   Time Concluded:

First Practice Observation

A. List each formal norm, and describe how it is communicated to people.

B. Describe behaviors associated with the formal norms.

C. What is the basis of your inference?

D. List each informal norm, and describe how it is communicated to people.

E. Describe behaviors associated with the informal norms.

F. What is the basis of your inference?

Decoding Human Behavior: Social Norms and Daily Life

Worksheet 2: Second Practice Observation (see instructions on p. 31)

Name: _____

1. Description of Social Environment:

2. Date of Second Practice Observation:

3. Time Begun:

   Time Concluded:

Second Practice Observation:

A. List each formal norm, and describe how it is communicated to people.

B. Describe behaviors associated with the formal norms.

C. What is the basis of your inference?

D. List each informal norm, and describe how it is communicated to people.

E. Describe behaviors associated with the informal norms.

F. What is the basis of your inference?

Decoding Human Behavior:
Social Norms and Daily Life

Worksheet 3: Field Study I (See instructions on p. 31)

Name: _____

1. Description of Social Environment:

2. Date of Field Study I:

3. Time Begun:

   Time Concluded:

Field Study I Observation

A. List each formal norm, and describe how it is communicated to people.

B. Describe the obedient behavior associated with formal norms.

C. What is the basis of your inference?

D. Describe any deviant behavior associated with formal norms.

E. What is the basis of your inference?

F. List each informal norm, and describe how it is communicated to people.

Worksheet 3, Continued

Name: _____

    G. Describe the obedient behavior associated with informal norms.

    H. What is the basis of your inference?

    I. Describe any deviant behavior associated with informal norms.

J. What is the basis of your inference?

K. Diagram the spatial organization of the environment.

L. Describe the physical and sensory properties of the environment.

M. Which behaviors do you find most predictable? Why?

Decoding Human Behavior: Social Norms and Daily Life

Worksheet 4: Field Study II (see instructions on p. 31)

Name: _____

1. Description of Social Environment:

2. Date of Field Study II:

3. Time Begun:

   Time Concluded:

Field Study II Observation Period

A. List each formal norm, and describe how it is communicated to people.

B. Describe the obedient behavior associated with formal norms.

C. What is the basis of your inference?

D. Describe any deviant behavior associated with formal norms.

E. What is the basis of your inference?

F. List each informal norm, and describe how it is communicated to people.

Worksheet 4, Continued

Name: _____

    G. Describe the obedient behavior associated with informal norms.

    H. What is the basis of your inference?

    I. Describe any deviant behavior associated with informal norms.

J. What is the basis of your inference?

K. Diagram the spatial organization of the environment.

L. Describe the physical and sensory properties of the environment.

M. Which behaviors do you find most predictable? Why?

Understanding Social Location

Andrea Malkin Brenner, American University

Rationale

People, especially Americans, have a habit of looking at others' worlds as they look at their own. Sociologists use something called the *sociological perspective* or the *sociological imagination* as a tool that enables them to gain a new vision about social life. The sociological perspective/imagination allows sociologists (and students of sociology) to temporarily step outside of their "bubble" and look at other people's cultures as well as their own.

A more specific element of the sociological perspective is the concept of *social location*, which explains "where" people are located in history and in a particular society (e.g., income, education, gender, race, ethnicity, and age). The concept of social location allows us to study people in different places and even in different time periods.

As we go about our daily routines, we often forget that our lives are in many ways affected by larger, seemingly invisible forces. Once we can grasp the concepts of the sociological perspective/imagination and social location, we have the ability to study people more objectively and learn from their experiences, even if those experiences vary greatly from our own.

Instructions

1. Take approximately 10 minutes to carefully read the excerpts on the next two pages.

2. When finished, complete the reaction questions.

3. As a class, you will talk about the social location of each of the narrators to clarify the content.

4. Share your feelings in a class discussion, using your written reaction as a starting point.

Grading

This is usually an ungraded classroom assignment, although you are all required to participate. Check with your instructor for his or her grading details.

Excerpt One

Americans want to have everything sanitized. No smells! Not even the good, natural man and woman smell. Take away the smell from under the armpits, from your skin. Rub it out, and then spray or dab some nonhuman odor on yourself, stuff you can spend a lot of money on, ten dollars an ounce, so you know this has to smell good. "B.O.," bad breath, "Intimate Female Odor Spray"—I see it all on TV. Soon you'll breed people without body openings.

I think white people are so afraid of the world they created that they don't want to see, feel, smell, or hear it. The feeling of rain and snow on your face, being numbed by an icy wind and thawing out before a smoking fire, coming out of a hot sweat bath and plunging into a cold stream, these things make you feel alive, but you don't want them anymore. Living in boxes which shut out the heat of the summer and the chill of the winter, living inside a body that no longer has a scent, hearing the noise from the hi-fi instead of listening to the sounds of nature, watching some actor on TV having a make-believe experience when you no longer experience anything for yourself, eating food without taste—that's your way. It's no good.

The food you eat, you treat it like your bodies, and take out all the nature part, the taste, the smell, the roughness, then put the artificial color, the artificial flavor in. Raw liver, raw kidney—that's what we old-fashioned full-bloods like to get our teeth into. In the old days we used to eat the guts of the buffalo, making a contest of it, two opposite ends, starting chewing toward the middle, seeing who can get there first; that's eating. Those buffalo guts, full of half-fermented, half-digested grass and herbs, you didn't need any pills and vitamins when you swallowed those. Use the bitterness of gall for flavoring, not refined salt or sugar. *Wasna*— meat, kidney fat and berries all pounded together—a lump of that sweet *wasna* kept a man going for a whole day. That was food that had the power. Not the stuff you give us today: powdered milk, dehydrated eggs, pasteurized butter, chickens that are all drumsticks or all breast; there's no bird left there.

You don't want the bird. You don't have the courage to kill honestly—cut off the chicken's head, pluck it and gut it—no, you don't want this anymore. So it all comes in a neat plastic bag, all cut up, ready to eat, with no taste and no guilt. Your mink and seal coats, you don't want to know about the blood and pain which went into making them. Your idea of war—sit in an airplane, way above the clouds, press a button, drop the bombs, and never look below the clouds—that's the odorless, guiltless, sanitized way.

Source: From John (Fire) Lame Deer, *Lame Deer Seeker of Visions,* 1972, New York: Washington Square Press, pp. 110–111.

Excerpt Two

"Don't buy anything from a filthy Jew," said Ilse as she read to Hans from one of his storybooks. "'Remember, my child, what Mother has told you.'"

Sitting next to Ilse on the living room couch, Hans clapped.

"Did you like that, Hans?" said Ilse, hugging him.

"You read very well, Ilse," I said, smiling at her over my glass of cognac. "Doesn't she read well, Marta?"

"Yes," she said, knitting. "Read Daddy the first part, Ilse, the part you read to me while I was fixing dinner."

Ilse flipped through the pages, a pensive look on her face. The Christmas wreaths filled the room with the scent of pine. The shiny paper of the wrapped packages piled under the tree reflected the fire's light. The red sweater Marta was making covered her knees, and she rested her hands atop it. Hans, wearing his pajamas, waited patiently beside Ilse, his small hands folded on his leg. Ilse stopped turning the pages and smiled.

The German is a proud man, A worker and a fighter.

The German is a proud man, Beautiful and brave.

The German is a proud man Who hates the dirty Jew.

And here is a Jew, as all can see. The vilest man that'll ever be.

"That's very good, Ilse," I said.

"She didn't understand what 'vile' was," said Marta, "until I explained it to her."

"Do you want to see the picture, Hans?"

Ilse leaned toward him and held the open book in front of him.

"Here's the beautiful German."

Hans clapped his hands.

"And here's the filthy Jew."

Source: From Sherri Szeman, *The Kommandant's Mistress,* 1993, New York: HarperPerennial, pp. 21–22.

Understanding Social Location

Worksheet

Name: _____

1. Why is the perspective of the writer important in each piece?

2. How do the writers' social locations explain certain aspects of human behavior and assumptions about the readings?

3. What if these readings are taken out of context?

4. How does the sociological perspective of this 80-year-old Sioux on a reservation and German children in WWII living next to a concentration camp take into account social location? Would you eat raw buffalo guts? Would you read this particular book to your children?

5. How would you describe your social location? How has it influenced your life? Do you think that your social location affected your reading of these pieces? If so, how?

Application Exercise on Ethnocentrism and Cultural Relativism

Virginia Teas Gill, Illinois State University

Rationale

One feature of the sociological perspective is that it sheds light on the relationship between culture and behavior. When we understand that different cultures have different norms for behavior, then it becomes easier for us to understand why people in different cultures act the way they do. Our feelings about the superiority or "naturalness" of our own culture's ways, however, can lead us to automatically judge unfamiliar cultural practices. Such judgment can act as a barrier to understanding; in effect, it blinds us to the social organization that is present in other cultures.

Suspending our own cultural assumptions and judgments can help us better understand other cultures, and it has the additional effect of helping us to see our own more clearly. We do not need to permanently shed our sense of what is right or wrong—for example, our views on human rights. That is, if we make an effort to set aside judgment for a while and try to see the world from the perspective of members of another culture, we will gain a richer understanding of their behavior and society.

The purpose of this exercise is to help you understand the difference between taking an ethnocentric view of a behavior and taking a culturally relative view of a behavior. This activity is a collaborative group exercise; you will write your own response to the questions, share your responses with other members of a four-person group, and construct a group response that is clearly superior to any of the individual responses.

Instructions

After reading the passage that follows these instructions, write your own response to the questions on the worksheet. You can refer to your textbook or notes for this assignment. Put your name at the top of the page.

When we indicate, break into groups of four. Read your individual answers to each other. Choose one group member to be a scribe. Redo the assignment with everyone contributing, and write one group response to the questions on a separate sheet of paper. As a result of your collaboration, the group response should be superior to any of the individual responses. Do not merely recopy one of the individual responses; to receive full credit, you must work as a group to improve upon the individual responses. Use complete sentences and check your grammar and spelling. Every group member must read and approve the group response before you hand it in. Print the name of each group member at the top of the group response.

When finished, each group should turn in all four individual responses with the group response stapled on top.

Grading

See your instructor for details regarding how this exercise will be graded.

Read the following passage:

> In 1997, Annette Sorensen, 30, an actress from Copenhagen, Denmark, and Exavier Wardlaw, 49, a movie production assistant from Brooklyn, NY, were arrested for leaving their 14-month-old daughter outside a Manhattan restaurant on a chilly day while they ate inside the restaurant. They left the child in her baby carriage on the sidewalk. Many passersby called 911 to alert the police. New York authorities took the child away from her parents and temporarily placed her in foster care.
>
> In an ensuing article in the *New York Times,* one Danish commentator observed that leaving a baby outside of a restaurant is a very common practice in Denmark. The commentator wrote, "Often, Danish parents. . . leave their babies outside. For one thing, Danish baby carriages are enormous. Babies ride high above the world on horse-carriage-size wheels. It's hard to get such a carriage into a cafe. . . . Besides, Danish cafes are very smoky places." The commentator continued, "In Denmark, people have an almost religious conviction that fresh air, preferably cold air, is good for children. All Danish babies nap outside, even in freezing weather—tucked warmly under their plump goose-down comforters. . . . In Denmark all children own a sort of polar survival suit that they wear from October to April and they go out every day, even in winter."

Application Exercise on Ethnocentrism and Cultural Relativism

Worksheet

Name(s): _____

1. Define ethnocentrism.

2. Define cultural relativism.

3. In a paragraph, write an ethnocentric interpretation of the parents' actions.

4. In a paragraph, write a culturally relative interpretation of the parents' actions.

Peer Learning in Sociology

Learning About Other Cultures From International Students

Beth Pamela Skott, University of Bridgeport

Rationale

This assignment is designed to supplement what you are learning in your textbook and lectures about other cultures. It is so hard to understand concepts such as polygamy and arranged marriages if you have never experienced them or been exposed to them in your own culture. You will learn only so much from the textbook, so this is an excellent opportunity to expand your knowledge. In this exercise, you will interview students from other cultures about their cultural practices, which should complement and reinforce what you have already learned from the textbook.

The first thing you need to know is that every single one of my students in previous classes dreaded this assignment until they actually did it, so if you are a bit concerned, you are not alone! Students came up with countless reasons why they could not participate. However, after the exercise, they all commented on how much they learned and how much they enjoyed the assignment.

Instructions (a.k.a. How To Make This Project Your Own)

Group work and careful planning are essential to this project. Each group will take one chapter (or one section of a chapter) from the text material. Every group member will need to read this chapter carefully (especially since you may be doing the exercise before your professor has a chance to lecture on it)! The main goal is to come up with a series of questions about the topic to ask the students from other countries. You need to be very careful when forming these questions. They need to be phrased carefully and clearly. Remember that although these students will have a good grasp of the language, English is not their first language. You may find that you need to further clarify your questions when actually conducting the interview, so be prepared to explain the concepts in other terms as well.

As you are creating your questions, you should keep in mind that the answers you receive are likely to prompt you to think of more questions.

Do not feel that you need to stick to the prepared list of questions—I find this exercise works best when students are casual and relaxed, rather than rigidly sticking to a "script" or interview schedule. Opening up a discussion rather than using only your previously prepared questions can enhance the experience for both your group and the other students. Your instructor will provide additional information on the interview process.

Class Presentation and Paper

Once your interview is complete, you need to start preparing a presentation for your class, as well as a paper. This will require your group to meet at least once (most likely two or three times) outside of class. Your presentation is crucial to helping your classmates learn how other cultures approach your topic. The more thorough and complete your presentation, the better your class-mates' understanding. Generally, there are two ways to structure your presenta-tion—by topic and by country. You might have each student in your group take one topic from your text and explain how each culture approaches it, or you might have each student take one culture/country and explain how that culture approaches each of the topics.

Some questions to keep in mind throughout this exercise:

1. How do the practices of the different cultures differ from your own? How are they similar?

2. Taking any judgments you might have out of the picture, can you see the pros and cons of the different cultural practices?

3. Are there any practices you originally saw as "odd" but now would be willing to accept?

4. What would you have liked to learn more about, if you had the chance to do this exercise again?

5. What advice do you have for groups that have not yet visited the other students/classroom?

    And, most important . . .

6. How does all of this relate to sociology?

One component of this project that can be the most difficult is coming up with appropriate questions. Your questions need to be phrased clearly but not in a way that you are talking down to the other students. Your biggest concern with the questions is to phrase them clearly (understanding that this may require rephrasing them) and that they are not judgmental.

Don't Ask . . .	Instead Try . . .
Why is abortion illegal in your country?	What does a woman do if she gets pregnant and is not married or does not feel ready to have a baby?
Why can't you marry anyone you want?	How are marriages arranged in your country? What happens if you are unhappy with the choice?

You will use Worksheets 1 and 2 to help you identify topics and social practices on which you would like to focus in your interviews and develop possible interview questions on these topics.

Grading

Please see your instructor for grading information for this assignment.

Peer Learning in Sociology—Learning About Other Cultures From International Students

Worksheet/Brainstorming Sheet 1

Name: _____

What is the name of the textbook chapter to which you have been assigned?

What is the main topic in this chapter that you want to explore? Are there any other topics in the chapter that interest you?

What are some subtopics that might relate to the main topic?

How are these topics examined in your culture?

> **Brainstorming Notes**
> In this space write down as many words as you can think of that are related to your topic.

How do you expect them to differ in other cultures?

Other notes:

Peer Learning in Sociology—Learning About Other Cultures From International Students

Worksheet/Brainstorming Sheet 2

Name: _____

In the space below, list the key words you and your group came up with. Next to each key word, write one sentence to describe how it fits into your culture. Below this, start to brainstorm interview questions. What would you like to know about other cultures?

Observing Culture

Craig This, Sinclair Community College

Rationale

Culture can be defined as the language, beliefs, values, norms, behaviors, and material objects that are passed from one generation to the next. Typically, culture is divided into material culture and non-material culture. The material culture is the objects that distinguish a group of people, such as their art, buildings, weapons, utensils, hairstyles, clothing, and jewelry. The non-material culture is a group's way of thinking (including its beliefs, values, and other assumptions about the world) and doing (its common patterns of behavior, including language and other forms of interaction).

At the end of this assignment, you will be able to do the following:

Identify values, norms, mores, folkways, language, symbols, and technology

Perform a direct observation

Instructions

For this assignment, you will visit one of the eating establishments on campus. During your visit, you will observe the culture of the establishment and use the table provided below to provide two or three examples of each. In your observation, you may observe the food service workers only, the customers only, or a combination of the two.

While it is possible for there to be an overlap between categories, it is asked that you provide different examples for each category. Both folkways and mores are norms, but do not list a norm from the norm category as either a folkway or more. Instead, please find a different folkway or more to use for their respective categories. A definition of what you are observing is provided along with an example.

Grading

See your instructor for details on grading this exercise. Generally, each example that you provide will be graded as to how well it matches the definition for the particular category in which you have placed it.

Observing Culture

Worksheet

Name/Names of Members in Group: _____

Place Observed: _____

Time: _____ Day of Week (circle one): Su M T W Th F Sa

Category	Examples	
Values: the standards by which people define what is desirable or undesirable, good or bad, beautiful or ugly.	Example: cleanliness	Two examples of values (1) (2)
Norms: expectations, or rules of behavior, that develop out of values.	Example: wait in line	Two examples of norms (1) (2)
Folkways: norms that are not strictly enforced.	Example: saying "please" and "thank you"	Two examples of folkways (1) (2)
Mores: norms that have great moral significance.	Example: not stealing food	Two examples of mores (1) (2)
Symbol: something to which people attach meaning and that they then use to communicate.	Example: $	Two examples of symbols (1) (2)
Language: a system of symbols that can be put together in an infinite number of ways and can represent not only objects but also abstract thought.	Example: the word "coffee"	Two examples of language (1) (2)
Technology: knowledge that people use to make a way of life in their surroundings.	Example: coffee maker	Two examples of technology (1) (2)

3

Socialization, Interaction, and Group Influence

Writing Children's Books

Peter Kaufman, State University of
New York at New Paltz

Rationale

Most of us grew up reading children's books. In addition to aiding in our literacy development, these books also taught us many social, cultural, moral, and even political values. When we read these books as children (and even as adults), we may not be aware of the embedded and oftentimes subtle messages that are being conveyed to us. By thinking sociologically about children's literature, we are more likely to realize that these books are not merely innocent stories that entertain us; rather, they are important components of our social, cultural, moral, and political socialization.

This exercise is intended to get us thinking about how knowledge is constructed through children's books. As you go through the exercise, you will be challenged to consider what content is appropriate for what age groups and how such content should be conveyed. You will also need to think about the implicit and explicit themes that are contained within children's books. By understanding children's books from a more critical and sociological framework, you will gain insight into one of the mechanisms through which we are socialized to accept the prevailing norms and values of society.

Instructions

The class will be broken up into groups of three or four students. Each group will write the text of a children's book based on the issue that is assigned to your group. You should discuss what information about this issue you want to include, as well as how you want to convey this information to the readers. In determining what the content of your book will be, you should identify the age group for which your book is being written. You do not have to draw pictures (although you can if you want). After each group has written their book, we will read the books out loud and each group will explain the content and style of their story. Please have someone in the group write the story on the back of one of the worksheets to hand in at the end of class.

Grading

See your instructor for details concerning how this assignment will be graded.

Writing Children's Books

Worksheet

Your name: _____

Names of Group Members: _____   _____

_____   _____

Your group will be assigned a number that corresponds to one of the issues below. Your task is to write the text of a children's book based on this issue. Circle your assigned issue.

1. Slavery in the United States
2. The events of September 11, 2001
3. War
4. Sexism
5. Racism

6. Non-heterosexual family structure
7. Global poverty
8. Poverty in the United States
9. Immigration
10. Aging and death

A. To what age group will your book be directed?

_____ Pre-School Years (Ages 3–5)

_____ Early School Years (Ages 6–8)

_____ Older Children (Ages 9–12)

B. Explain why you chose this age group.

C. List 7–10 possible topics related to this issue that you *might* include in the text of your book.

D. In the space below, or on another piece of paper, write the text of your children's book.

Gender Socialization

Betsy Lucal, Indiana University at South Bend

Rationale

The purpose of this exercise is to give you a chance to analyze how children learn about gender. This exercise will help you put what you have learned about socialization and/or gender into practice. It will give you a sense of how social structures and institutions are organized, created, and maintained in society. It will help you understand how children learn to "do gender" (in other words, to behave and present themselves in ways that make them easily viewed as a boy or as a girl). By analyzing how children's toys and/or clothes are "gendered" (in other words, organized into categories appropriate for boys or girls), you will have a chance to see how gender and socialization work in the real world.

Instructions

1. In preparation for the group portion of the assignment, you will need to visit a department, children's clothing, or toy store so that you can observe the items offered for sale.

2. While you are at the store, pay attention to how clothing and/or toys are organized. How do you know which items are intended for boys/girls? Make a list on the worksheet of the kinds of items intended for boys/girls. Are there any gender-neutral or non-gendered items (i.e., items that would be appropriate for both girls and boys)? Make a list of them. (Refer to the worksheet for more information about what to look for when you observe.)

3. Come to class ready to participate in a group discussion about your observations.

4. With your group, answer the following questions. Each member of the group should take a turn writing down an answer to the question.

   A. Compare group members' findings from their observations. What patterns do you see? Did anyone find anything unusual or unexpected?

   B. What kinds of things do you think clothes and toys teach children about gender? How do they teach them to be a boy or a girl? Think about the kinds of clothes and toys your group determined to be appropriate for each gender and how the clothes might affect, for example, a child's movements or how the toys might affect, for example, a child's interests.

C. Based on your group findings with respect to clothing and toys, what does it mean to be a boy or a girl? What kinds of messages do clothes and toys provide children about what it means to be a boy or a girl? In other words, what do boys and girls look like, act like, enjoy doing, and so forth?

D. Are there any ways in which toys and clothing encourage girls and boys to be similar to each other? Explain.

E. Spend some time talking about how group members decided which toys/clothes were appropriate for boys versus girls and which ones were gender-neutral. What does this tell you about your own gender socialization?

F. If we are being sociologically mindful, then these findings must be taken a step farther. We cannot stop with the patterns. We have to think about what they mean and how these patterns connect with other aspects of the social world. On one hand, these observations show that we use gender as a way to organize the social world. Discuss what this concept means. On the other hand, gender is not just a matter of differences between groups of people. Gender, in our society, is a basis for inequality—for assigning people different roles, rewards, responsibilities, and so forth. Discuss how children's toys and clothing can perpetuate (maintain) this form of inequality.

5. After class, write a reaction paper. What did you learn from this group exercise? How much of an impact do you think children's clothes and toys have on gender socialization and the perpetuation of gender inequality? Do you think parents realize what kinds of effects the toys and clothes they buy for their children can have on them? Will the findings from this activity influence the toys and clothes you buy for the children in your life?

6. Turn in your worksheet, the notes from your group discussion (only one copy of these needs to be turned in from each group), and your reaction paper.

Grading

You will likely be graded on the thoroughness of your worksheet notes, on the quality of your group's responses to these questions, and on the thoughtfulness of your reaction paper. Please see your instructor for details on grading.

Gender Socialization

Worksheet

Name: _____

Name of the store where you observed: _____

    I observed (circle one) TOYS   CLOTHING   BOTH

    How can you tell which toys/clothes are for girls versus boys?

    If you're observing clothes, pay attention to and describe . . .

    The items of clothing offered for

        BOYS

        GIRLS

        BOTH

The fabrics/clothing textures used for

        BOYS

        GIRLS

        BOTH

The patterns/decorations used for

> BOYS

> GIRLS

> BOTH

Other differences between clothes for

> BOYS

> GIRLS

Are there any gender-neutral clothes (in other words, clothes that appear to be for either a boy or a girl)? Describe them.

If you're observing toys, pay attention to and describe . . .

The kinds of toys offered for

> GIRLS

> BOYS

> BOTH

The colors, designs, and so on for

> GIRLS

> BOYS

> BOTH

Any other differences between toys for

> GIRLS

> BOYS

Leadership, Gender, and the Invisible Ceiling*

Survey Activity

Keith A. Roberts, Hanover College

Rationale

This is a survey exercise in which you gather data from about 25 students—male and female—that allow us to reflect on social conceptions of masculinity and femininity and our society's definitions of leadership. Understanding that our definitions of "leadership characteristics" tend to correspond very highly to our society's definitions of masculinity can help us understand forces that help to create the *invisible ceiling*.

Instructions

1. On page 81, you will find a "Characteristics of Leaders" sheet.

2. Photocopy this sheet (make 25 copies).

3. Ask 25 men and women (roughly an equal number of each, if possible) to fill out your sheet. Ask them to follow the instructions on the sheet, explaining that this is a survey for a class and that the results will be anonymous (do not ask for names on the sheet). Do *not* tell them that this is a study of gender or of the invisible ceiling. If they ask, tell them it is a survey on the qualities that Americans look for in leaders—which is true.

4. When all sheets have been completed, shuffle them so you will not know who might have filled out each sheet. Then add up the number of answers for each category of response.

5. Divide the number of answers for each item by the total number of sheets that were completed (probably 25). This will give you the percentage of respondents who felt the characteristic was a leadership quality.

Excercise adapted from an unknown author

6. Place the percentage figure for each trait in the appropriate blank on the worksheet and bring the sheet to class. The scores for Masculinity and Femininity were developed by having several hundred college students at a liberal arts college complete a form that looked identical to the sheet you have photocopied, with one exception. The instructions at the top looked like this:

Masculinity and Feminity

Mark each characteristic with an "M" or an "F" depending on whether you think it is generally defined by society as a masculine or feminine characteristic.

In my experience, the list of gender characteristics generated by using this survey is highly correlated to the list of preferred leadership qualities that you are likely to have found from your surveys regarding leadership. I usually find around 12 to 14 "direct correlations" between masculinity and leadership. I usually find 3 to 5 "inverse correlations" (masculinity high and leadership low *or* masculinity low and leadership high; as a benchmark, use "*above* 57%" as a "high" score and "*below* 43%" as a "low" score). For example, if 93% of your respondents thought "achiever" is a leadership quality and 71% of those already surveyed think it is a masculine quality that would be a positive correlation to leadership. If 11% of your sample thought that "devious" is a leadership quality and 73% think it was masculine, then there is an inverse or negative correlation between masculinity and leadership.

The interesting question is how the correlation of "masculinity" and "leadership" might unwittingly cause a woman to be overlooked for promotion on the job or poorly evaluated if she is in a leadership position. If a woman is "masculine," it often makes people uncomfortable with her. On the other hand, if she is not "masculine" (as our society thinks of it), she may be thought of as a person lacking leadership qualities.

Grading

See your instructor for details on grading. If your instructor asks for a written paper, you will write an essay (two to three double-spaced typed pages, plus the data summary sheet) in which you will explain the patterns you found in your data and what they mean. If, indeed, the qualities we define as "leadership" qualities correspond to the qualities that our society happens to define as "masculine," you should discuss how that might impact women in the workplace. How might that help to explain why women encounter an *invisible ceiling* (an unconscious or unwitting form of sexism)? How might your findings from your survey indicate a pattern that leads to the statistics in the table titled "Income by Educational Level and Sex"?

Include as an appendix to your paper your sheet that shows the scores. The audience for this paper should be other college students who do not know anything about the concept of an "invisible ceiling."

Criteria for grading will be (1) ability to interpret the data from the survey in a clear manner, (2) ability to explain the concept of the invisible ceiling, (3) ability to explain and illustrate concrete ways in which our definitions of leadership and of masculinity may disadvantage women, often without awareness of the bias by any of the people making the decisions, and (4) control of the conventions of good writing so as not to jeopardize your credibility with the reader.

Income by Educational Level and Sex

Education	*Men*	*Women*
Not a High School Graduate	$28,345	$16,075
High School Graduates	40,119	23,143
Some College; No Degree	48,812	26,720
College Graduate (Bachelor's)	71,140	40,200
Master's Degree	85,700	48,535
Doctorate	105,928	73,516
Professional Degree	148,611	72,592

Source: From *Statistical Abstract of the United States*, 2005.

Characteristics of Leaders

Mark an "X" by the 10 characteristics that you think are the essential qualities for a **leadership** position in a complex organization (business, government, etc)

____ achiever

____ aggressive

____ analytical

____ caring

____ confident

____ dynamic

____ deferential (defers to others; yields with courtesy)

____ devious

____ intuitive

____ loving

____ manipulative

____ nurturing

____ organized

____ passive

____ a planner

____ powerful

____ sensitive

____ strong

____ relationship-oriented (makes decisions based on how others will *feel*)

____ rule oriented (makes decisions based on *abstract procedural rules*)

Leadership, Gender, and the Invisible Ceiling: Survey Activity

Worksheet

Name: _____

	Leadership Trait	Masculine Trait	Feminine Trait
Achiever	____%	71%	29%
Aggressive	____%	99%	1%
Analytical	____%	58%	42%
Caring	____%	1%	99%
Confident	____%	96%	4%
Dynamic	____%	69%	31%
Deferential (defers to others; yields with courtesy)	____%	7%	93%
Devious	____%	73%	27%
Intuitive	____%	12%	88%
Loving	____%	3%	97%
Manipulative	____%	65%	35%
Nurturing	____%	1%	99%
Organized	____%	12%	88%
Passive	____%	0%	100%
A Planner	____%	27%	73%
Powerful	____%	99%	1%
Sensitive	____%	3%	97%
Strong	____%	96%	4%
Relationship-oriented (decisions based on how others will *feel*)	____%	3%	97%
Rule oriented (decisions based on *abstract procedural rules*)	____%	87%	13%
Total: Direct Correlations with Leadership	____	____	____
Total: Inverse Correlations with Leadership	____	____	____

NASA

Understanding Social Interaction

Heather M. Griffiths, Fayetteville State University

Rationale

This exercise will introduce you to sociological concepts related to society and social interaction. You will pretend that you are an astronaut, one member of a crew that has crash-landed 200 miles away from your original landing point on the light side of the moon. In order to survive, you must rank the 15 items not damaged in the crash in order of most important (1) to least important (15). The survival of the crew depends on your ability to decide successfully which items are the most important and indispensable for your 200-mile journey, and which you might safely discard in order to lighten your load.

Instructions

This is a two-part exercise. First, you will receive up to 15 minutes to rank the 15 items listed on your individual exercise sheet. When this task is complete, four to six students will volunteer for further participation. These students will leave the room and read their instructions while the rest of the class receives further instructions from the professor. Following these separate instructions, the class volunteers return to the classroom and conduct Part II of the exercise.

In Part II, the student volunteers will work together to create a master list ranking the supplies in order of importance. To begin this part, the student volunteers will introduce themselves to the class. These students must reach a consensus on a final list; they may vote on their final list only three times. Your professor will then match this final list against the official answers. When the group rankings are different from the official rankings, the professor will note the difference, ignoring whether the difference is plus or minus. Finally, your professor will add the differences in ranking to determine your final score.

Grading

See your instructor for details on scoring and grading. One way to do this follows. If the student volunteers are within 25 points of the correct answers, they succeed and the entire class gets full credit for the exercise. If the volunteers are within 50 points of the correct answers, the entire class will receive half credit. If the volunteers score more poorly than that, no one will receive any credit for the assignment.

NASA: Understanding Social Interaction

Individual Worksheet

You are a member of a space crew originally scheduled to rendezvous with a mother ship on the lighted surface of the moon. Due to mechanical difficulties, however, your ship was forced to land at a spot some 200 miles from the rendezvous point. During landing, much of the equipment aboard was damaged; and since survival depends on reaching the mother ship, the most critical items available must be chosen for the 200-mile trip. Below are listed the 15 items left intact and undamaged after landing. Your task is to rank order them in terms of their importance to your crew in allowing them to reach the rendezvous point.

Place the number 1 by the most important item, the number 2 by the second most important, and so on, through number 15, the least important. You have 15 minutes to complete this phase of the exercise.

____ Box of matches

____ Food concentrate

____ Fifty feet of nylon rope

____ Parachute silk

____ Portable heating unit

____ Two .45 caliber pistols

____ One box of dehydrated milk

____ Two 100 lb. tanks of oxygen

____ Stellar map (of the moon's constellation)

____ Life raft

____ Magnetic compass

____ Five gallons of water

____ Signal flares

____ First aid kit containing injection needles

____ Solar-powered FM receiver-transmitter

NASA Group Instructions

Please leave the room while I give the rest of the class their instructions. Do not talk to each other while outside of the room.

Your group must reach a consensus on what is most important. You will come to this consensus in front of the class. When you have finished, you will write your final answer on the Master NASA sheet. You must come to a consensus by discussing your choices. You can make up to three votes before choosing your final list.

Your answer is then scored against the NASA approved Master List, and if you score below 25 points on the Master List, you and each of your classmates will receive full credit for this assignment. If you score between 25 and 50 points, you all receive half credit.

If you score 51 or more points, no one will receive credit for this exercise.

Understanding Social Interaction

Master Worksheet

You are a member of a space crew originally scheduled to rendezvous with a mother ship on the lighted surface of the moon. Due to mechanical difficulties, however, your ship was forced to land at a spot some 200 miles from the rendezvous point. During landing, much of the equipment aboard was damaged; and since survival depends on reaching the mother ship, the most critical items available must be chosen for the 200-mile trip. Below are listed the 15 items left intact and undamaged after landing. Your task is to rank order them in terms of their importance to your crew in allowing them to reach the rendezvous point.

Place the number 1 by the most important item, the number 2 by the second most important, and so on, through number 15, the least important. You have 15 minutes to complete this phase of the exercise.

_____ Box of matches

_____ Food concentrate

_____ Fifty feet of nylon rope

_____ Parachute silk

_____ Portable heating unit

_____ Two .45 caliber pistols

_____ One box of dehydrated milk

_____ Two 100 lb. tanks of oxygen

_____ Stellar map (of the moon's constellation)

_____ Life raft

_____ Magnetic compass

_____ Five gallons of water

_____ Signal flares

_____ First aid kit containing injection needles

_____ Solar-powered FM receiver-transmitter

Group Decision Making

Judy L. Singleton, College of Mount St. Joseph

Rationale

This exercise was developed to help you in your sociology courses to experience the processes that people encounter in group decision-making situations rather than merely to read about them. The assignment will also help you to apply sociological concepts and give you the opportunity to discuss decision-making issues in a group format.

Instructions

Your instructor will assist you with forming groups. The groups are likely to be the same as in one or more of your previous group exercises.

1. A recorder is to be selected before beginning the discussion and written analysis.

2. Based upon your previous experiences doing work in the groups, each group will discuss, analyze, and answer the questions on the worksheet provided. All group member names are to be listed on the top of the worksheet.

3. Each member *individually* is to answer on the separate worksheet why he or she would rather do class work within a group structure or why he or she would prefer not to do class work within a group structure. What are the benefits versus the disadvantages of group work? This section is to be submitted individually on the separate worksheet by each group member with that group member's name written on the top of the sheet. This section is not to be submitted on the group answer sheet.

Grading

See your instructor for details regarding how this exercise will be graded.

Group Decision Making

Worksheet

Group Members' Names:

Discuss and answer the following questions as a group.

1. How were roles assigned to members in the group projects? Be specific as to the type of roles in each group and why people elected to participate in those roles.

   A. Who emerged as the leader during each project? Why?

   B. What type of leaders did your group have?

   C. Discuss why others permitted individuals to accept certain roles.

   D. Did different people assume different roles in different group projects? Discuss why this situation might or might not have occurred.

2. What affected the participation of members? Did everyone participate equally?

   A. How did the size of the group affect decision making?

   B. How did knowing or not knowing other group members impact the group decision-making process?

C. Consider the composition of the group. How heterogeneous or homogeneous was your group? Did this situation impact decision making in any way? Explain.

3. How was a group decision made? Were there concerns about conforming, expressing different opinions and ideas, being subject to "groupthink," and so on? Explain why.

    (Use extra paper as needed, and append your paper to the worksheet.)

Group Decision Making

Worksheet—Individual Assessment of Group Decision Making

Name: _____

Individually answer the following questions (use the back of the page as needed):

1. Would you rather do class work within a group structure, or would you prefer not to do class work within a group structure? Indicate which you prefer and why.

2. What are the benefits versus the disadvantages of group work?

3. Reflect here on what you have gained from analyzing group decision making as a social process in this group decision-making exercise.

4 Stratification

Six Statements for Teaching Social Stratification

Lissa J. Yogan, Valparaiso University

Rationale

The following exercise will be used to help illustrate the power of ideology, and achieved and ascribed characteristics, in assigning responsibility for the vast economic disparity present in the United States.

By the end of the two class periods, you should have a better understanding of economic inequality, the ways in which ideology is shaped by our ascribed and achieved characteristics, and the ways in which one's life experiences are shaped by the large social categories of gender, race, and class.

Instructions

Please complete the following sheet individually. Simply circle the answer that comes closest to accurately representing your beliefs. There are no right or wrong answers and you will not be graded on what you circle.

1. After you circle your answers, you can begin to think about the reasons you chose *agree* or *disagree* for each statement. You will be placed into a group and given time to talk about each statement and each person's response.

2. After your group meets and discusses the statements, please come to consensus and write down a group answer (agree or disagree) for each statement. If your group has trouble agreeing on an answer, take notes about why people could not find common ground.

3. Once you have completed these steps, please have one group member come to the front of the room and write your group's consensus answer for each statement on the overhead.

4. Once you have written down your group's answers for each statement, proceed to discuss the four questions at the end of the worksheet. Designate one student to be the official recorder. This student will summarize your group's answers to these questions on the back of the worksheet.

5. When we have all the groups' responses to the six statements recorded, we will examine them as a whole and talk about the reasons groups may have arrived at different answers.

6. The answers to the four questions you record on the back of the worksheet will be handed in at the end of class and discussed in the next class.

7. At the end of the second class, you will be asked to individually type a paper that answers the same four questions (found in Part III of the worksheet) your group answered. This paper is due on _____. (Check with your instructor regarding a grading rubric that may be used to evaluate your paper.)

Grading

The assignment will be graded on a pass/fail basis. On day two, when you hand in your group worksheet, please place a check mark by the name of any group member who did not contribute to your group discussion.

1. If you provide answers on your final individual paper that met the criterion listed for "passing answers on the grading rubric" and you participated, then you will receive a passing grade.

2. If you did not participate, you will not receive a passing grade.

3. If you do not write answers that earn a passing mark for each of the four questions, you will be asked to re-do the questions. You must receive a passing grade on all questions by your second attempt in order to pass this assignment.

Six Statements for Teaching Social Stratification

SOCIAL STRATIFICATION IN THE UNITED STATES

Worksheet—Part I

Part I: Indicate whether you agree or disagree (circle the A or D) with the following six statements:

A   D   1. It is natural for some people to have a great deal more money and resources than others in our society.

A   D   2. The poor could improve their own situation if they made the needed effort.

A   D   3. Wealthy people will do everything they can to stay wealthy—and they can get away with it.

A   D   4. Everyone in our society has the opportunity to have a good standard of living.

A   D   5. It's not what you know but who you know that will help you get ahead in this world.

A   D   6. Talent and hard work usually pay off, no matter who you are.

Six Statements for Teaching Social Stratification

SOCIAL STRATIFICATION IN THE UNITED STATES

Worksheet—Parts II and III

Part II: You will be placed in a small group. In your group, discuss your individual answers to the above six statements. As a group, reach consensus on an answer (either agree or disagree) for each of the statements. Put your group answers below:

1. _____   3. _____   5. _____
2. _____   4. _____   6. _____

Part III: Now, as a group answer the following questions based on your own thoughts and the discussion that occurred in your small group:

Usually, not all group members agree on the above statements. Given that fact:

1. Among your group members, what factors contributed to different views on the same question?

2. What role do ascribed factors play in your answers (either your own ascribed characteristics or the assumed characteristics of those referred to in the questions)?

3. What role do achieved characteristics (yours or those you assume about people/groups in the question) play in your choice of agree or disagree on each of the six statements?

4. What do you think is the biggest cause of economic inequality in the United States?

Have a group member summarize your discussion on the next page. List the names of your group members after you write up the group answers to these questions.

Answers to Questions in Part III:

Group# ____

Names	*Did not participate*		*Did not participate*
_____	[ ]	_____	[ ]
_____	[ ]	_____	[ ]
_____	[ ]	_____	[ ]

Guided Fantasy

The Titanic Game

John R. Bowman, University
of North Carolina at Pembroke

Rationale

This exercise is designed to introduce you to the topic of social stratification, or social inequality in society. This guided fantasy is based on events that actually happened a few minutes before midnight on April 14, 1912. On her maiden voyage to New York, the luxury ocean liner *Titanic* struck an iceberg in the North Atlantic. Of the more than 2,200 passengers and crew onboard, only about one-third survived. Similarly, you find yourself on a smaller ship that is about to sink. In the case of the *Titanic* only 30% of those onboard survived; therefore, only 4 of the 12 individuals on your boat will survive. Although the actual sinking of the *Titanic* took nearly three hours, this group activity will be conducted in about 30–50 minutes.

Instructions

1. You are on a luxury liner and the ship's captain announces the following message. "Please do not panic! The ship has just hit an iceberg and we are about to sink. Unfortunately, there is not enough room on the lifeboat to save everyone. Because we won't sink for at least another twenty minutes, we must decide who among us will be saved. Only four of us will survive."

2. Each person in the group will be assigned a number that will correspond to the following person or occupation:

   1. Retired person
   2. Ship's captain
   3. Physician
   4. Nurse
   5. Migrant worker
   6. Welfare mother (or father)
   7. U.S. Senator
   8. President of the *Titanic* ship line
   9. President's spouse
   10. President's baby
   11. U.S. Army captain
   12. Elementary school teacher

3. Begin this activity by first identifying yourself to the other group members. Tell them who you are and try to convince them why **you** should be allowed to get on the lifeboat. Remember that everybody wants to live and you are fighting for your life!

4. After the introductions and appeals, each group must decide how it will make its decision as to who is to survive.

5. The group should then discuss who should be permitted to get on the lifeboat. Keep in mind that each person selected for the lifeboat means one less seat for you.

6. After completing this group exercise, individuals should then answer each of the discussion questions on the "*Titanic* Game Worksheet."

7. Be prepared to provide the instructor a list of the survivors and share your answers to the worksheet discussion questions with the rest of the class.

Grading

See your instructor for details on grading this exercise in your class. Often the grade will be based on the level of your participation in this group activity. You should actively assume the role of your assigned position and you should actively participate in the discussions and deliberations. You should provide a thorough description of the events that took place in your group, as well as answer the other discussion questions.

Guided Fantasy: The *Titanic* Game

Worksheet

Name: _____

Discussion Questions

1. Who were the survivors selected by your group?

2. How did you personally reach a decision on who you thought should survive?

3. In your group deliberations, what were some of the comments made about some group members?

4. Are there certain people in society who are more important than others? If so, who are they? Do you believe that this was a consideration in your group's choices of who should live and who should die?

5. Are there situations in real life where life-and-death decisions are made about people solely on the basis of their position or occupation? Provide examples.

Food Stamp Challenge

Sandra Enos, Bryant University

Rationale

In the United States, we are facing a significant problem with food insecurity, which means that many families and their children face the prospect of not knowing where their next meal will come from. We have a system of public benefits, one of which is the Food Stamp Program. Many individuals believe that food stamps provide enough food for families to make it through an average month with enough food to sustain them. In this exercise, you will test this out for yourself. Consider when you are doing this exercise whether you have resources that poorer members of the community may not enjoy, for example, transportation to the market of your choice, ability to buy in bulk, enough cash to take advantage of sales, and so on.

Instructions

Food stamps provide support for families and individuals who meet income and other qualifications. Review a typical application for food stamps and public assistance at the http://www.ridhseligscreening.org/English/FS.pdf website. Consider how "simple" it is to apply for benefits. You can also use a quick tool to see if you are eligible for food stamps. This is available at http://65.216.150.143/fns/.

In this assignment, you will assume that you have a weekly food stamp allotment of $42 for yourself and your nine-year-old son or daughter. (The national average food stamp allocation for one individual is $21 per week.) Take a trip to your local grocery store and see if you can plan a week of meals for yourself and your child on the food stamp budget. You can dine out if you'd like, just try to stay within the food stamp allotment. Make certain you allot yourself the amount of food you typically eat. The serving portion on packaging may not match your own consumption patterns.

You can also do this online by visiting your local online grocery delivery service. The web address shown below is an example of one of these.

http://www.peapod.com/index.jhtml

What you should outline below is your weekly food plan. For example,

Purchases	Costs
A gallon of milk	3.99
12 oz Cap'n Crunch	3.99
7 Bananas @ .30 each	2.10
I lb spaghetti	1.19
I jar spaghetti sauce	3.29
2 potpie chicken (6 servings)	12.00
English muffins	1.29
2 meals Chili at Wendy's with sodas. . . . and so on	8.00

Then prepare a week's menu, estimating how far these groceries will take you. Include your incidental purchases, as well, like a cup of coffee or snacks or a special treat for your child.

Example

Day one

Breakfast: 1 serving Cap'n Crunch with milk, English muffin

Lunch: 2 servings can of soup

Dinner: 2 servings potpie

Grading

See your instructor for information about grading this exercise. Common criteria, however, include your completion of all aspects of the assignment and your linking of course concepts addressed in readings and in class discussions to this assignment.

Food Stamp Challenge

Worksheet

Name(s): _____

Purchases	Costs	Estimated # of servings
Total	$	

Continue on reverse if you need more space.

Day One

    Breakfast _____

    Lunch _____

    Dinner _____

Day Two

    Breakfast _____

    Lunch _____

    Dinner _____

Day Three

    Breakfast _____

    Lunch _____

    Dinner _____

Day Four

    Breakfast _____

    Lunch _____

    Dinner _____

Day Five

    Breakfast _____

    Lunch _____

    Dinner _____

Day Six

    Breakfast _____

    Lunch _____

    Dinner _____

Day Seven

    Breakfast _____

    Lunch _____

    Dinner _____

Report

In a two-page report, discuss your findings. Was this relatively easy to do? What were the challenges of living within a food stamp budget? What strategies help to stay within your budget? Are the cheapest foods the most nutritious? What did you not purchase that you usually do? If you used a budget like this for an entire month, when would you expect to run out of food? What would you do then? Did you account for the fact that you may not have the resources that you are accustomed to, such as transportation, access to credit, and so on?

Making Ends Meet

Mellisa Holtzman, Ball State University

Rationale

Making ends meet may be more difficult than you think. This exercise will give you insight into the cost of living in the United States. That information will then be a starting point for discussing a number of key sociological concepts, including social class and poverty.

Instructions

Imagine a family of four living in your hometown. Assume that both parents work and that one child is 7 years old and in elementary school while the other is 3 and must be cared for during the day. On the worksheet is a list of all the goods and services this family will likely need or want in today's society. Your task is to work with a partner to estimate the ***monthly*** cost of each item. For some items, the family will incur most expenses all at once rather than each month (i.e., unlike school lunches, school supplies are purchased largely in August). Likewise, household expenses fluctuate considerably each month (i.e., holiday months are more expensive than others, etc.). For items such as these it may be easier to estimate a yearly cost and then divide that by 12 to get your monthly estimate. If you have trouble estimating the cost of an item, your instructor can assist you.

Grading

See your instructor for details about how this assignment will be graded.

Making Ends Meet

Worksheet

Names of Group Members: _____

$ (taxes and insurance included)

    Groceries _____

    Car payment _____

    Car gas _____

    Car insurance _____

    Electricity _____

    House gas _____

    Water _____

    Garbage collection _____

    Cable/Satellite TV _____

    Internet _____

    Home phone _____

    Cell phone _____

    Student loans _____

    Credit cards _____

    Medical insurance _____

    Life insurance _____

    Mortgage _____

    Child care _____

        (For 3 yr. old as well as afterschool care for 7 yr. old)

    School supplies _____

        (Lunches included)

    Entertainment _____

        (eating out, movies, video rental, etc.)

Household expenses _____

> (toilet paper, paper towels, birthday and holiday gifts, car repairs, clothing, shoes, etc. This is a very large category; think hard about your estimates!)

Monthly Total _____

Yearly Total (monthly × 12) _____

   amount of money the family would need to bring home after taxes (net)

Gross Income (yearly × 1.25) _____

   amount of money the family would need to make before taxes, assuming a 25% tax bracket (multiply by 1.15 for a 15% tax bracket)

1. What social class would this family need to belong to in order to meet these expenses?

2. Notice that this budget does not account for monthly savings. Recalculate your totals to include $200 per month contributed to a savings account. How much additional money would the family need to earn per year (gross income) to meet this savings goal?

3. The poverty line for a family of four in 2006 was $20,794 per year. Recalculate your estimates assuming the family is in poverty. How can their costs be decreased? What goods and services will they have to do without in order to live on less than $21,000 per year?

Global Inequality

Comparing Guinea to the United States

Fadia Joseph and Donal J. Malone,
Saint Peter's College

Rationale

This assignment is designed to help you understand global inequality and its impact on the life chances of people living in developed and less developed countries. In the process, we explore the sociological perspective and how it illustrates how our lives are shaped by the society we are raised in. In addition, this assignment's purpose is to explore the causes of global inequality.

Instructions

Part I

Go to the following website on the Internet and do the following: https://www.cia.gov/library/publications/the-world-factbook/index.html

1. Select the country of Guinea. Read all of the information listed about Guinea.

2. Based on what you read, select three of the following categories:

   Geography

   People

   Government

   Economy

   Communications

   Transportation

   Military

   Transnational Issues

3. From each of these categories choose one fact or statistic that made an impact on you and write a one-page reaction paper explaining why.

Part II

1. On the same website select the United States. Read all of the information listed about the United States.

2. Choose the same three categories for the United States that you chose for Guinea. Compare the two countries with regard to the same information. (For example, if you chose "infant mortality rate" for Guinea, you should compare it to the infant mortality rate in the United States.) In a one-page reaction paper, discuss similarities or differences you found in comparing these facts or statistics. In other words, what do these facts or statistics tell you about each country, the lifestyle of its people, and their chances in life? Provide examples in your answer.

Grading

See your instructor for details regarding how this exercise will be graded.

Global Inequality:
Comparing Guinea to the United States

Worksheet 1

Name: _____

GUINEA

Category 1 _____

Choose one fact or statistic that made an impact on you and explain why.

_____

_____

_____

_____

Category 2 _____

Choose one fact or statistic that made an impact on you and explain why.

_____

_____

_____

_____

Category 3 _____

Choose one fact or statistic that made an impact on you and explain why.

_____

_____

_____

_____

Global Inequality:
Comparing Guinea to the United States

Worksheet 2

Name: _____

United States

Category 1 _____

Similarities or differences:

_____

_____

_____

_____

Category 2 _____

Similarities or differences:

_____

_____

_____

_____

Category 3 _____

Similarities or differences:

_____

_____

_____

_____

Global Inequality:
Comparing Guinea to the United States

Worksheet 3

Name: _____

In a one-page reaction paper, discuss similarities or differences you found in comparing these facts or statistics. In other words, what do these facts or statistics tell you about each country, the lifestyle of its people, and their chances in life? Provide examples in your answer.

Global Stratification and Its Impact on a Country's Population Characteristics

Edward L. Kain, Southwestern University

Rationale

Global stratification has a wide variety of consequences for individuals who live in any country. For example, citizens in a wealthy developed nation experience a much higher standard of living that leads to lower infant mortality and higher average life expectation.

This assignment allows you to explore some of the variation in population characteristics that is related to inequality between nations. To do this, you will use a data source that includes information not only on the United States, but on every country in the world—the website of the United States Census Bureau.

We will discuss this assignment in class, so it is important that you bring it with you on the day it is due.

The assignment has two simple goals—to introduce you to a source of international demographic data that you might find useful in sociology and other classes, and to have you start thinking about how to use demographic data to understand a society and compare it to other societies.

Instructions

The instructions are included on the worksheet starting on page 127. As noted on the worksheet, using the International Data Base at the website for the United States Bureau of the Census, you need to:

1. Choose two different countries—a developed (high-income) country and a developing (medium- or low-income) country.

2. Print the "Summary Demographic Data" for each of these two countries and bring that to class with you for discussion.

3. Write three paragraphs, one each addressing the questions on the worksheet.

4. Come to class prepared to discuss these data.

Grading

See your instructor for information about grading this exercise in your course.

Global Stratification and Its Impact
on a Country's Population Characteristics

Worksheet

Name: _____

For this assignment:

I. Go to the International Data Base at the Census Bureau: http://www.census.gov/ipc/www/idb

II. Click on "Country Summary."

A. From the pull-down list, choose a developed country—a high-income country. Print the results and bring them with you to class.

1. Choose a developing country, either a middle-income or a low-income country. Print the results and bring them with you to class. If you need help choosing countries at these different levels of development, a general rule of thumb is that countries in North America (the U.S. and Canada) and Western Europe are high-income developed countries. In addition, Australia, New Zealand, Japan, North Korea, and Taiwan are also high-income developed countries. On the other end of the spectrum, many of the countries in sub-Saharan Africa are among the poorest in the world. Data on per capita income and other measures of the economy can be found at the World Bank Website of World Development Indicators: http://devdata.worldbank.org/wdi2006/contents/Section1.htm

Name of the developed country you chose:

What other countries did you look at before making this choice?

Name of the developing country you chose:

What other countries did you look at before making this choice?

What influenced your decision to make these choices?

B.   Attach your printouts to this sheet. Use them to do the following:

  1. Write a paragraph in which you compare and contrast the basic demographic measures listed at the top of the printouts—in particular, compare and contrast the two countries in terms of **current** crude birth rate, crude death rate, annual growth rate, life expectancy at birth, infant mortality rate, and the total fertility rate.

  2. Write a second paragraph in which you briefly compare the two countries in terms of how these measures are expected to change between this year and 2025. Which of the two countries is expected to have more change in its demographic characteristics?

  3. Write a paragraph in which you describe the shapes of the population pyramids in the two countries and also talk about how their shapes **and sizes** will (or will not) change from this year to 2025.

On the day that we discuss this in class, hand in both the printed data sheets and your answers to these questions. Please have them stapled together (or at least make certain your name is on all sheets).

5

Organizations, Bureaucracy, and Work/Occupations

Team Case Study of a Community Organization

Rebecca Bach, Duke University

Rationale

Throughout the semester we examine a number of serious social problems, so by the end of the semester you may feel discouraged about the human condition. In this project you will have the opportunity to become familiar with social problems in the local community and to begin to envision potential solutions to social problems. The assignment is designed to enhance your ability to apply course concepts and theories to the real world and to develop your research and analytical skills.

Instructions

Each team will identify a local community organization that addresses one of the social problems we have studied this semester. For instance, if you are interested in family violence, you could study a local domestic violence shelter. If interested in drug abuse, you could study the DARE education program in schools, or a local rehabilitation program. Your research should include examining the organization's website and any of the organization's publications, such as newsletters or brochures. In addition, you are expected to conduct interviews with some combination of the following populations: employees of the organization, volunteers of the organization, and/or clients of the organization.

The final team project should include each of the following components:

1. An introduction that offers a brief overview of the project and includes your research questions.

2. An explanation of the purpose and goals of the organization and the larger social problem that the organization addresses.

3. A discussion of the theoretical underpinnings of the organization's work on this social problem. For example, is a conflict theory implicit in the organization's mission and goals?

4. A summary of the organization's programs and the populations they address.

5. An evaluation of the effectiveness of the organization in accomplishing their goals. How do the clients of the organization evaluate its programs? How do the staff members evaluate the effectiveness of its programs? What do they consider a "success story"? What do they see as the major challenges they face? What would they like to do differently?

6. Recommendations for improving organizational effectiveness.

Grading

Ask your instructor to explain the grading criteria.

Team Case Study of a Community Organization

Worksheet

Team Members' Names:

Complete the following during class and turn in to me before you leave.

1. What organization are you going to study?

2. What social problem does it address?

3. What sources of information will you use?

4. Who will be primarily responsible for obtaining information from each source? (In other words, what is your division of labor?)

5. What questions will you ask in your interviews? Don't worry about the final phrasing of the questions at this point, but think about what you want to learn from each question.

For clients:

For staff:

For volunteers:

Structural Change at Your College or University

Charles S. Green III, University
of Wisconsin at Whitewater (Retired)

Rationale

The college or university that you attend is a complex organization—a bureaucracy. Its structure is an ongoing pattern of relations characterized by specialized occupations and coordinated and controlled by a hierarchy or administrators. Why does the structure exist, and what makes it change? The objective of this exercise is for you to find answers, albeit partial ones, to this question.

Instructions

Your instructor will assign each group, or ask each group to volunteer, to answer *one* of the questions on the worksheet. All questions involve gathering information, and the information for most questions can be assembled from the two organization charts that your instructor will provide. Groups will share their findings in class and discuss their implications.

Grading

Check with your instructor on grading criteria, but how thoroughly and accurately you complete the assignment will no doubt influence your grade.

Structural Change at Your College or University

Worksheet

Group # _____

1. How much growth in the administrative component of your college or university has taken place?

	Number of Positions		Change	
Positions	Year 1	Year 2	Number	Percentage
Top dogs	_____	_____	_____	_____
Others	_____	_____	_____	_____
Total	_____	_____	_____	_____

Group # _____

2. Why has growth taken place?

   a. Has the number of students grown? Has the number of faculty grown? (Make use of the library to find out.)

   b. Could there be other (externally induced) reasons for growth? (Refer to the *Journal of Higher Education* article for possible reasons.)

Group # _____

3. Was there a change in the gender composition of administrators? If so, why did it occur?

For example:

   a. Were more women than men recruited to new positions? (This situation might indicate that new positions were created for women to make the institution look good.)

b. Were more women than men recruited to old positions? (This situation might indicate genuine efforts to stop gender discrimination.)

c. Both?

	New Positions	Old Positions	
		Year 1	Year 2
Men	_____	_____	_____
Women	_____	_____	_____
Vacant positions or gender indeterminate	_____	_____	_____
Total	_____	_____	_____

Group # _____

4. What sorts of structural changes have taken place? Describe the changes that have taken place (offices added or dropped and changes of titles). Speculate—in a disciplined way—why the changes took place. (If needed, use an additional sheet of paper for your answer.)

Critique of Student Government

Alton M. Okinaka, University of Hawai'i at Hilo

Rationale

The political philosophy of the United States of America is based on democratic principles, taking the form of a republic. As a participatory form of government, it integrates public opinion and power into elections. These elections assume an informed public that will select candidates based on their performance and character.

A common theme in public discourse is the weaknesses of this system and questions about the efficacy of such a system. Does this system in fact empower the masses or simply provide the illusion of power? To what degree are the premises of an informed public true, and is this concern the cause of many of the problems in government? Many people express the opinion that their vote does not really matter, and voter apathy would seem to be a direct reflection of this attitude. Yet, the amount of money spent on campaigns and advertising to shape public opinion would suggest that there is power in the system.

For most Americans, politics is something that they rarely get involved in directly. On those occasions when an issue is of concern for them, most Americans do not know how to get involved and make an impact on the decision-making process. Even in our education systems, we teach about American history and the structure of American government and the electoral process, but we rarely cover how people can get involved or influence decision making. While it seems that most Americans love to talk about (and complain about) American government at all levels (county, state, and federal), we rarely discuss what would characterize a good government or how to affect this result.

The purpose of this assignment is to raise your awareness of the democratic political process and have you reflect on what you would want from your government.

While it might be difficult to gain access to resources in order to properly investigate the civil governments at the county, state, or federal level, there is a level of participatory government at most colleges and universities that is, or should be, readily available to all students. This government is the student government at your school. Most colleges and universities have a student government that serves to represent the student body, much in the same way as elected officials at the county, state, and federal levels represent their constituencies. A portion of the student fees that you pay goes to student government as the equivalent of taxes. Since you are the constituency of your elected student government, those who are elected have an obligation to represent you and your interests.

Similar to elections at other levels, participation on college campuses varies greatly, with many student bodies demonstrating high levels of apathy. Many of the characteristics of American politics that are complained about at all levels exist as well on the college campus. This government provides a local resource for students to learn about the process of electoral and representative politics and hopefully to develop some insights into what makes it work and why (and how members of the public can get involved and make a difference).

Consider aspects such as the purpose, procedures, organizational rules, openness to input from their constituency, ability to work with the college administration or other agencies, dissemination of information to their constituency, and effectiveness of your student government. In all of these aspects, consider not only what it does well but also its weaknesses and how things might be improved.

Instructions

Form groups of four to six students. By working in groups, you will have more opportunities to collect information and to compare impressions and ideas.

Discuss and outline your ideal vision of what your student government should be doing and how. This vision will serve as the basis for a critique of the student government in operation by comparing what they are actually accomplishing and how with your expectations. In forming this vision, you should consult sources such as the constitution and bylaws of your student government as a basis of their formal charge and prescribed procedures. Such material is often available on your campus website.

Collect information about what the current student government's goals are, how it is conducting business, and what it is achieving. In performing these actions, consider both the process by which it operates and the consequences. Effectiveness and efficiency are often linked but are not always identical. Coordinate your information-gathering efforts with your group mates.

Critique and discuss the information gathered. In performing this critique, match up the ideals of the institution in its formal documents, such as the constitution and bylaws, your own vision for how it should operate, and the information that you collected about how the government actually operates. Consider how efficient and effective it is, the appropriateness of its goals and procedures, and the degree of conflict and/or cooperation that takes place. You should consider not only how it deals with issues that you were initially concerned with but also whether it is dealing with issues you had not anticipated. Consider its strengths, weaknesses, and how it could improve.

Write a group report on your critique. Provide your vision and how it matches with the formal goals and rules of the student government as well as how this then matches its actual operation and your recommendations for improvement.

Present a summary of this report in class, and compare your report to reports done by other groups.

While many sources of information are available, here is a short list of possibilities to help you get started:

- student government constitution, bylaws, and operating rules
- minutes of meetings and bills and resolutions
- interviews with members of student government
- interviews with members of the administration who deal with student government
- interviews with students who are represented by the student government
- articles in papers or news stories about student government activities
- information about student governments at other schools for comparison

Grading

See your instructor for information about grading this exercise in your course.

Critique of Student Government

Worksheet

Group members

Name: _____   Phone Number: _____   E-Mail: _____

Name: _____   Phone Number: _____   E-Mail: _____

Name: _____   Phone Number: _____   E-Mail: _____

Name: _____   Phone Number: _____   E-Mail: _____

Name: _____   Phone Number: _____   E-Mail: _____

Name: _____   Phone Number: _____   E-Mail: _____

Name: _____   Phone Number: _____   E-Mail: _____

Vision of goals for student government:

Sources of Information:

Information about actual goals and procedures:

Critique:

Occupation and Income Exercise

Keith A. Roberts, Hanover College

Rationale

This exercise was designed to help you think about the reward systems in our society and the reasons for inequality of rewards for various occupations. Why do we pay more for some jobs? Are these reward systems fair? Do they help the society, or do they in some ways create problems? Why do we think as we do about the differential in pay for various lines of work?

Instructions

On the following page you will find an "Occupation and Income" sheet. In groups of about four or five members, determine what you think would be appropriate levels for each of the listed occupations, with the total for all occupations not to exceed $500,000. This should not take more than 20 minutes or so.

When you finish, give a copy of your answers to the instructor. The instructor will then lead a discussion about the scores and after the discussion you may be asked to write a short analytical paper.

Grading

See your instructor for his or her plans for grading this exercise. If the instructor asks for a written paper, you will submit an essay (2–3 double-spaced typed pages) in which you will explain how inequality in the society is functional and how it is dysfunctional. Use concrete examples from the list you worked with and illustrate your essay by discussing discrepancies in pay for various occupations. The audience for this paper should be other college students who do not know the two sides of the argument.

Criteria for grading will be (1) your ability to articulate clearly and accurately the functionalist argument about inequality in society, (2) your ability to articulate clearly and accurately the conflict argument about social inequality, (3) clarity in the use of examples, and (4) control of the conventions of good writing so as not to jeopardize your credibility with the reader.

Occupation and Income

Worksheet

Name: _____

Your task is to decide how much income a person in each of the following occupations ought to receive. You will want to consider justice (fairness) and practicality (what will "work") as you distribute income based on a fixed or limited pool of resources.

You have *$500,000* total to distribute to the following *male* workers:

_____ 1. Physician

_____ 2. Loan officer

_____ 3. Medical scientist

_____ 4. Garbage/Refuse collector

_____ 5. Elementary/Middle school teacher

_____ 6. Telecommunications equipment installer

_____ 7. Bus driver

_____ 8. Jailor/Correctional officer

_____ 9. Food service manager

_____ 10. Emergency medical technician (EMT)

_____ 11. Farm laborer or fisherman

Fast Food, Fast Talk

Interactive Service Work

Catherine Fobes and Adam Gillis, Alma College

Rationale

As service workers, service recipients, or as managers, Interactive Service Work (ISW) impacts us on a daily basis. Therefore, it is important to understand its components and complexities. This exercise on McDonald's was developed to help you learn about and apply the components of ISW, enact varying alignments of the components, and discuss your experiences as participants and observers.

Instructions

Review and discuss the "Social Dynamics in Interactive Service Work" chart with your instructor, then fill out Part I of the worksheet. Your instructor will ask for students to volunteer, and he or she will choose half of the number of students needed for the skit. The other half of the participants will be chosen from the student body that did not volunteer. This way there will be a mix of students who volunteered and who did not. Those of you not in the skit will serve in the role of observers.

As skit participants, you will be assigned to your various positions as manager, burger-flippers, window workers, and service recipients; as observers, please pay careful attention to how actors enact the varying alignments of *A and B versus C*, etc., as seen in the chart on the "Social Dynamics in Interactive Service Work."

After the exercise, record your reactions to the skit in Part II of the worksheet.

Finally you will be encouraged to discuss your experiences as participants, as well as your observations as audience members.

Grading

See your instructor for information on the grading of this exercise in your course.

Social Dynamics in Interactive Service Work

Social Dynamics	Example Scenario
A and C versus B =	Service worker treats service recipient rudely or inappropriately. Service recipient approaches manager who warns service worker.
A and B versus C =	Service recipient orders a lot with no money to pay for it. Window worker asks for and receives manager's support. Manager asks service recipient to leave.
B and C versus A =	Service worker gives "unapproved" order to service recipient on the sly without manager's knowledge.

Source: Adapted from P. Y. Martin, lecture on "Complex Organizations," Florida State University, 1995.

Fast Food, Fast Talk: Interactive Service Work

Worksheet

Name: _____ Date: _____

Part I—Past Experiences

1. Have you ever worked in this type (Interactive Social Work) of position?   **Y**   **N**

2. If yes, what job(s) did you perform?

3. If yes, how did you feel about the job or position that you held?

Part II—Reactions and Reflections

1. How does this exercise show the concept of Interactive Service Work (ISW) to you?

2. How did you feel and react to being the various characters in different situations?

3. If you were assigned a specific character, from where did you draw your inspiration to portray him or her?

4. How might an understanding of ISW help you in your daily life? In your future career?

6 Race and Gender

Thinking Critically About Race Through Visual Media

Marcia Marx and Mary Thierry Texeira,
California State University, San Bernardino

For manipulation to be most effective, evidence of its presence should be nonexistent. When the manipulated believe things are the way they are naturally and inevitably, manipulation is successful. In short, manipulation requires a false reality that is a continuous denial of its existence. It is essential, therefore, that people who are manipulated believe in the neutrality of their key social institutions. They must believe that government, the media, education, and science are beyond the clash of conflicting social interests.

—Herbert Schiller from *The Mind Managers* quoted in Michael Parenti, *Make-Believe Media: The Politics of Entertainment* (St. Martin's Press, 1991).

Rationale

The above quote reflects the goal of this assignment: to examine how the *process of socialization* through the media and other sources influences our beliefs and values about many aspects of society, including about groups that are unlike our own cultural group. Sociology has given these processes much attention, especially as it examines how the media shape the nature of public information, images, and ideologies. If we examine how we learn about other groups or social phenomena, the result would likely include visual media. Indeed, studies confirm that most of us get our information about social phenomena from television and film.

In this assignment you are asked to examine the *process* that shapes our understanding of "the other" (groups perceived as culturally different from our own group). Since we are interested in the ways that perceptions are shaped in our society, we can examine how negative and positive representations of non-whites in U.S. television programming influence the nature of public debate. This will be a group project that your members will present in class during the last week of the term. The goal of this assignment is to increase our awareness of both the overt and more subtle, covert messages about race and ethnicity that are embedded in television programming and feature films.

The most damaging visual images and messages about various groups are those that are negative but appear "natural" and therefore go uncontested. For example, women and men in television commercials have highly gendered roles. Men are seen as mostly working outside the home and women inside. Men are rarely shown in domestic settings, that is, pushing a vacuum cleaner, changing babies' diapers, or serving food to their wives and children. If, indeed, fathers are shown feeding the family, the wife is absent and he is serving fast food or microwavable fare. Therefore, while such commercials are not explicitly about gender relations (they are selling products), their portrayal of women in the home and men in the public sector reinforces traditional gender divisions and sends very subtle messages about gender. Moreover, such commercials reinforce the "normality" of traditional gender roles by ignoring the role of women in the labor market and men's domestic labor, including care of their children.

Usually the visual media are not specifically about race, gender, or other forms of inequality. For example, if you were interested in identifying unspoken assumptions that reinforce gender inequality, a film like *The Hours* would not be a good choice of film to use in this exercise on gender because in it, gender and sexual identity are critiqued and are the main focus of the film. There are better examples of the *subtle, covert* messages about gender if you examine action or adventure movies because in these genres, gender inequality begins with "manly" men and supporting roles for women.

The preceding examples discuss some of the gender coding of commercials and action films that occurs in media. In a similar way, we would like you to examine race and ethnicity in various television programming and feature films to show how both overt and subtle, covert messages influence the development of stereotypical beliefs and attitudes about racial and ethnic groups.

Instructions

There are two parts to this assignment.

Part I

Randomly assigned groups will prepare a five-minute video for in-class presentation. The video will consist of several clips based on one of the following types of visual media accessed from television. Each group will have one of the following categories:

1. News program
2. Documentary
3. Music video
4. Sports program
5. Cartoon
6. Situation comedy
7. Magazine show
8. Commercial
9. Contemporary (post-1990) feature film
10. Talk show

Video clips that your group collects and presents should depict distortions of race/ethnicity based on stereotypical and inaccurate assumptions about various groups. The particular show or film that you use should *not* be about race or ethnicity. That is, you would not choose a clip from a film like *Malcolm X* as an example because the film is specifically about race and racism. Remember, as in the above quote, the most harmful messages are those that appear natural and ordinary. So, automobile commercials that always show the Asian characters doing karate chops might be something that you will want to consider. Why? They embrace the stereotype of Asians as martial artists to the exclusion of all other images.

The following procedures facilitate the completion of this project, especially the class presentation portion:

1. Once the instructor has assigned groups, members should exchange phone numbers and e-mail addresses.

2. Groups should meet with the instructor in class to determine the exact definition of their particular visual media category. That is, if your assignment is "news magazines," then everyone in the group should have a common understanding of what a news magazine is. The instructor will help to clarify meanings.

3. Each member should tape approximately 15 minutes of video clips from his or her particular category. This will mean that you may have to tape 3–4 hours of footage in order to get a few clips that meet your criteria. If you need assistance editing your presentation, the media center at the university will help. If you have access to two video or DVD recorders, you can edit the clips on your own.

4. Arrange for a convenient time for *all* group members to meet outside of class. You will obviously need to meet somewhere that has video equipment, either in someone's home or the campus media center. Show your clips to the group at this meeting for evaluation.

5. At the meeting, the group should choose the best clips from all of the submitted ones, keeping in mind the time limitations.

6. Again, you may edit tapes at the media center, but if the group has access to two video or DVD recorders, you can edit on your own. Some groups in the past have even added music to overlap the spoken word in their presentations. Others have removed the dialogue in the film altogether and added music to emphasize the power of the visual images without dialogue. Some groups have even excluded the sound altogether.

7. Prepare a five-minute presentation by editing and splicing together the clips chosen by group consensus.

8. Decide how you will make your class presentation. Determine who in the group will present which part of the presentation to the class. These assignments should be determined by group consensus. All members of the group should speak before the class.

9. Prepare other visuals like overheads, PowerPoint, and charts to introduce your title, titles of clips, and/or an outline of your theoretical argument to the class. Remember that you will be teaching for a few minutes and should therefore try to hold the class's attention with as much inventiveness as possible.

10. Arrange another group meeting to rehearse your presentation. Timing is crucial (see grading criteria) because the first five groups will present in class on the first day, followed by the last five during the next class meeting. Therefore, we urge you to go through the presentation paying particular attention to this criterion, saving at least one minute for questions.

Part II

The second part of this assignment requires that you each prepare a paper that analyzes the messages and social impact of your group's video material. Papers should be 5–6 pages long and contain the following standard headings: **Introduction, Literature Review, Findings, Discussion,** and **Conclusion**. Analysis of the film clips selected by your group should be the focus of your paper, thus making the paper an expanded, in-depth version of your oral presentation. The papers should not only "decode" the stereotypes, but also consider the context that perpetuates negative social images. Ask yourselves, whose perspective is being reinforced by these distortions? Which social interests are served by these misrepresentations? Your literature review should incorporate information from your class lectures and reading assignments to provide a framework for your analysis. Keep in mind that what is not said or shown in a video is just as telling as what is said or shown.

For example, in the seemingly harmless, light comedic film *Ferris Bueller's Day Off*, the protagonist, a high school student, spends an entire "ditch day" in the city of Chicago, a multicultural city if there ever was one. Yet Ferris and his friends, all WASPs, manage to avoid speaking to any people of color during that whole day. Given the locale of the film, how realistic is this? How and why did the filmmakers eliminate speaking roles for people of color in this film? And what does that say about the power of filmmakers to literally erase the other? Calling upon the literature and class lectures, these are the types of questions that need to be addressed in the paper.

Finally, we would like your input by way of an evaluation of the assignment. What is the value of assignments such as this one, including how it affects the way you view visual media? Is this assignment a model that can be used to evaluate media's depiction of other groups besides people of color? If you could, how would you change the assignment to make it a more effective tool of media evaluation? While papers are to be written individually, we encourage general discussion among group members before the actual writing of your papers. Papers are due on the day of the presentation.

Grading

Check with your instructor regarding the percentage of your term grade that this assignment will count. Of the total for this assignment, I typically grade 40 percent for the group project and 60 percent for the individual paper. The group project grade will be based on the following criteria: (1) clarity of the presentation, (2) the group's ability to remain within the time frame of 10 minutes total, (3) relevance of the clips to your topic, (4) participation by all members, and (5) response to class questions. Group members will all receive the same grade for the presentation part of the project.

Grades for individual papers will be based on the following criteria: (1) clarity of your writing, including spelling, grammar and punctuation; (2) a balanced statement of your thesis; (3) sound use of the literature and class lectures to support your thesis; (4) relevance of video clips to the topic; and (5) in your conclusion, an assessment of the value of the assignment, including how it has affected how you watch visual media. Papers are due on the same day as the class presentation.

Thinking Critically About Race Through Visual Media

Worksheet

Name: _____

As you begin to think about both parts of this assignment, it is crucial that you have a clear understanding of the kinds of examples we are looking for in your presentations and papers. We suggest that before you record anything, as you view television or videos, consider what you are watching with a critical eye and ear. Use the space below to make notes on the key questions; these will help prepare you for your group project and your analysis paper. Good luck and happy hunting!

1. How do media present people of color, that is, are the images positive or negative? Why are the images positive or negative? Which social interests are served by these representations? Do you suppose this depiction is intentional on the part of the filmmakers or is something else going on?

2. What effect(s) do these representations of people of color have on our feelings/attitudes/beliefs about members of racial/ethnic groups? What about our feelings/attitudes/beliefs about the women or GLBT individuals in these groups?

3. Why and how is critical thinking, especially with respect to the visual media, important for understanding race relations in the United States?

4. What effect did this assignment have on how you view media in regard to race/ethnicity and other similarly disaffected groups, such as gays and lesbians, poor and working-class people, the disabled, and so forth?

5. How would you alter this assignment to make it a more effective tool of media evaluation?

Drawing Pictures

Race and Gender Stereotypes

Jacqueline C. Simpson, Guilford
Technical Community College

Rationale

A stereotype is a type of prejudice called *cognitive prejudice*. It is an exaggerated belief associated with a specific group and a tendency to believe that almost anyone who belongs to that group will have a certain characteristic. Stereotypes can be positive or negative and might have some truth or might not. The problem with stereotypes is that it is *assumed* that members of a specific group will have a certain characteristic, whether they do or not. Stereotypes ignore or overlook individual assets.

Because stereotypes have a negative connotation, it is difficult for most people to admit that we all have them. The stereotyping process can work in two ways: the first and most common is that an image is seen and a label is automatically attached to the image. In the second process, a label is heard or seen and an image is generated. The following exercise illustrates this second process and shows how insidious and ingrained stereotypes can be.

Instructions

On the following worksheets, draw two separate pictures, one each of:

A pretty child

A bully

- Please make your pretty child and bully full-length drawings. That is, include a body, arms, and legs in addition to a head.
- If possible, use crayons, colored pencils, or markers for your picture.
- Give your pretty child and bully each a name.
- After drawing your pictures, see your instructor for further instructions.

Grading

Please check with your instructor regarding his or her grading policy. Grades or evaluations could be determined on the following criteria: completing the assignment, both the full-length drawing and giving the drawings their names; participating in class discussion about what you and other students drew; knowing the definition of stereotype and cognitive prejudice; and your ability to recognize a generalization as a stereotype.

Drawing Pictures: Race and Gender Stereotypes

Worksheet 1

Name: _____

To Do: On this sheet of paper, draw a picture of a pretty child. Write the name of this pretty child in the space provided at the bottom of the paper.

NAME OF PRETTY CHILD: _____

Drawing Pictures: Race and Gender Stereotypes

Worksheet 2

Name: _____

To Do: On this sheet of paper, draw a picture of a bully. Write the name of this bully in the space provided at the bottom of the paper.

NAME OF BULLY: _____

"Stump That Race" Game

Melanie D. Hildebrandt,
Indiana University of Pennsylvania

Rationale

This exercise is intended to improve and deepen your understanding of majority/minority group relations in American society beyond what the "textbook" says, by giving you a chance to learn about racial and cultural differences with your classmates. Sometimes the thought of talking about race in a mixed race setting can be scary and stressful. This exercise is designed to create a more relaxed and open atmosphere so you can learn about race and privilege from each other, while also providing concrete examples of sociological concepts (race, ethnicity, assimilation, biculturalism, etc.) and theoretical perspectives (e.g., W. E. B. DuBois's ideas on race and the color line).

Instructions

In your team's circle, generate a list of questions that you think students of a different "race" will not be able to answer. These questions should focus on cultural differences (music, food, slang/vernacular, leisure activities, customs, etc.). Everyone in your group should know the answer or be familiar with the cultural phenomenon in order for the question to be included on your list.

If you are concerned that a question might be offensive, ask your instructor for guidance. If you need help generating questions, think of things or places, activities, or sports where you have observed few people of different races.

Once each team has generated 10 questions, your instructor will begin the game. Remember that your team's objective is to stump the team of a different race and NOT to be stumped by them. Consult with your teammates before shouting out answers.

When the game and discussion are concluded, each of you will be asked to write a short reaction essay and reflect on what you have learned. Your instructor may ask that you connect specific examples to concepts and ideas discussed in lecture.

Grading

Your grade will be based on your active participation and engagement with this activity as well as your thoughtful completion of the written assignment. See your instructor for further details.

Stump That Race

Worksheet

Name: _____

Quiz Questions

1. In this space, draft some questions about your race/culture that you think members of another race cannot easily answer. Your goal as a team is to stump the team of another race.

2. Once the game is over and the class has discussed the exercise, use this space below to write your immediate thoughts and reactions to the game. How did you feel before the game began, and did your feelings change as the game progressed? What did you learn that you didn't know before, and what questions/answers were the most surprising to you? What does this exercise tell you about majority/minority group relations?

3. Outside of class, write a 300-word essay offering your reflections on the game, connecting specific examples to concepts identified by your instructor. Staple that essay to this worksheet and submit it next class.

A Group Exercise in Affirmative Action

Jacqueline C. Simpson, Guilford Technical
Community College

Rationale

In an attempt to equalize opportunity in the United States for those groups that had been disadvantaged, Congress passed the Civil Rights Act in 1964. Of particular importance to Affirmative Action are Title VI and Title VII of the Civil Rights Act. Title VI prohibits discrimination in federally assisted programs, including colleges and universities that typically accept and distribute federally funded grants and loans for students. Title VII prohibits discrimination in private and public employment. To emphasize Title VI and Title VII, President Lyndon Johnson issued Executive Order 11246 in 1965. It is this Executive Order that uses the words *Affirmative Action.*

Because of the legislation's controversial history, it is difficult to understand the complexities and realities of Affirmative Action in the United States. In fact, many colleges, universities, and businesses had difficulty understanding (and, consequently, implementing) Affirmative Action policies. When there is difficulty in understanding and implementing legislation, it is often left to the U.S. court system to delineate the exact nature of the law. That is what happened with Affirmative Action legislation. Companies implemented what they thought were appropriate guidelines; they were sued; and the cases worked their way through the U.S. court system. Specifically, the U.S. Supreme Court specified what Affirmative Action is and what it is not with the cases of *Bakke v. the University of California* and *Weber v. Kaiser Aluminum.*

The following exercise is designed to familiarize you with Titles VI and VII of the Civil Rights Act of 1964, Executive Order 11246, and the Supreme Court decisions that determined the development of specific Affirmative Action policies. In addition, this activity is designed to illustrate just how difficult it is to develop and implement an Affirmative Action policy.

Instructions

1. Read the relevant segments from the Civil Rights Act of 1964 and Executive Order 11246.

2. Form groups of four or five students.

3. Decide whether your group will portray university admission officers or personnel directors for a large aluminum corporation.

4. If you chose university admission officers, follow the instructions on the worksheet titled "University Admissions."

5. If you chose personnel directors, follow the instructions on the worksheet titled "Kaiser Aluminum."

6. Your goal, regardless of which sheet you choose, is to develop an Affirmative Action plan based on what you read in the Civil Rights Act of 1964 and Executive Order 11246. *This task is a very difficult thing to do, so give it your best try.*

7. After devising an Affirmative Action plan, decide which students you would accept if you chose "University Admissions," or decide who to promote if you chose "Kaiser Aluminum."

8. Compare your results with those from the real cases. Your instructor will lead you in this portion of the exercise.

Grading

This exercise is difficult and does not have any clear divisions between right and wrong answers. Nonetheless, there are particular features of your participation that could justifiably be graded. First, participate in the development of an Affirmative Action plan. While difficult, it can be done. Remember, companies and universities in 1965 had no more information than you to develop a plan, but they did it—so you can, too. Second, be ready to communicate your rationale for your Affirmative Action plan given the legislation that you have read. Third, your selections for promotion and/or admission should reflect the specific plan that you devised. Fourth, after the exercise is completed, you should know what Affirmative Action is and what it is not. Fifth and perhaps most important, be able to distinguish between quotas and racial preference.

Civil Rights Act of 1964

General description: Banned racial, ethnic, and sex discrimination in employment and union membership. Prohibited discrimination by privately owned business providing public accommodations, such as hotels, restaurants, and theaters. Strengthened enforcement provisions against discrimination in education.

Executive Order 11246

General description: Emphasized Titles VI and VII of the 1964 Civil Rights Act, specifically two important passages:

". . . will not discriminate against any employee or applicant because of race, color, religion, sex, or national origin . . . will take affirmative action to ensure employees are treated without regard to their race, color, religion, sex, or national origin."

". . . take affirmative action not to discriminate and to develop affirmative action plans, including goals and timetables, for good faith efforts to correct deficiencies in minority and female employment."

A Group Exercise in Affirmative Action

Worksheet 1

Names of Group Members:

University Admissions

Situation: Davis Medical Center at the University of California at Davis can accept only 60 percent of its applicant pool. It has a relatively diverse student body and has no past history of discrimination. The following 10 students have applied for admission, but only six can be accepted.

To Do: As the admissions committee for UC-Davis Medical Center, you have two responsibilities:

Develop an Affirmative Action plan based on the 1964 Civil Rights Act and Executive Order 11246.

Decide, based on your plan, which six of the following ten applicants you will accept for admission.

	GPA	MCAT	RACE	RECs
#1	3.0	970	African American	good
#2	3.3	990	Euro-American	good
#3	3.2	980	Chinese American	fair
#4	3.3	1090	Euro-American	fair
#5	2.7	950	African American	fair
#6	3.6	1040	Euro-American	good
#7	3.2	920	Mexican American	excellent
#8	3.4	1010	Euro-American	fair
#9	3.7	1000	Euro-American	good
#10	3.4	1020	Euro-American	good

A Group Exercise in Affirmative Action

Worksheet 2

Names of Group Members:

Kaiser Aluminum and Steel Company:

A Private Employer in Louisiana

Situation: Kaiser Aluminum and the United Steel Workers Union must decide which of the following employees will be promoted to management (supervisor positions). There are three supervisory positions open. Currently, there are no women or people of color in supervisory positions. The company admits that the reason for this under-representation is that women and people of color were once discriminated against by company personnel.

To Do: As the personnel committee, you have two responsibilities:

Develop an Affirmative Action plan based on the 1964 Civil Rights Act and Executive Order 11246.

Decide, based on your plan, who will be promoted to supervisory positions. There are currently three supervisory positions available and ten possible employees who have the required credentials.

	Skill Level	*Years Employed*	*Race*
#1	average	ten	Euro-American
#2	above average	eleven	Euro-American
#3	average	eight	African American
#4	above average	seven	Latino-American
#5	above average	twelve	Euro-American
#6	average	eight	Euro-American
#7	above average	nine	African American
#8	above average	seven	African American
#9	above average	twelve	Euro-American
#10	average	six	Mexican American

Analyzing the Social Construction of Gender in Birth Announcement Cards

Jacqueline Clark, Ripon College, and
Maxine Atkinson, North Carolina State University

Rationale

This exercise helps to illustrate some of the ways that gender is socially constructed. You will be asked to work in pairs and then analyze several birth announcement cards designed for new parents. Analyzing the cards will help you to understand better how gender is socially created and defined.

Instructions

The class will be divided into pairs. Each pair will receive an envelope that contains two birth announcement cards. Work with your partner to analyze the cards. Pay special attention to how the cards describe and depict boys and girls.

On the worksheet provided, record the words used to describe each gender. Also record the kinds of images used on the cards. What do these words and images tell us about how boys and girls "should" be?

After you have analyzed the cards in your packet, join another group and share your findings. Discuss similarities and any differences in the cards. What patterns do you notice in the cards? Finally, discuss how the cards help to illustrate how gender is socially and culturally defined. Be prepared to discuss your cards and your analysis of them with the rest of the class.

Grading

See your instructor for specific information on grading this exercise in your course. Common criteria, however, include grading your analysis of the birth announcement cards and how well you can apply your assigned reading to your group analysis.

Analyzing the Social Construction of Gender in Birth Announcement Cards

Worksheet

Name: _____

1. Carefully examine each of the cards included in your packet, and then record the information listed below for each.

Card	Is the card for a boy, a girl, or is it gender neutral?	What colors are used in the card?	What words are used to describe the child?	What images and pictures are used for the child?
#1				
#2				

2. Overall, how are the cards in your packet characterizing boys and girls? In other words, what are the cards saying about how boys and girls "should" be?

3. Once you are finished with your packet, find another group that is also finished. Share your cards with each other, and look for common themes in them. Write notes of your analysis in the space below. Then, on a separate sheet of paper, write one short paragraph on behalf of the group describing (1) the common themes in the cards defining what a boy or girl should be and, (2) how these cards reflect your assigned reading. That is, based on your analysis of these cards, what have you learned about what we teach parents about gender and how we teach parents these lessons. Put all group members' names on the paragraph. You will hand your paragraph in before the class discussion.

Reading *Little Critter*

Understanding the Power of Symbols

Jacqueline C. Simpson,
Guilford Technical Community College

Rationale

As a type of non-material, intangible culture, a symbol is anything that communicates meaning between two people. One little object can transmit a number of different messages. A ring, for example, can signify the relationship status of an individual, particularly if it is a solid band or one with a diamond. Without saying a word, individuals who wear this type of jewelry on the ring finger of their left hand tell everyone in our society that they are not available for dating. The ring saves time and energy for everyone: An interested person will not waste words initiating a romantic encounter; the ringed person does not have to expend energy by repelling unwanted suitors. As suggested by this example, symbols simplify the existence for those of us who live in complex societies.

Because they require a minimum of two people to be exchanged, symbols are social entities: They are created by the group and reified by the group. A social entity that has meaning for just one person is not a symbol. For example, if students earn a grade of "Q" in a class, they have no idea what this means: Was my academic performance of a "quality" standard? Or does this mean my behavior was "questionable"? This social aspect of symbols, the need for a sender and a receiver, is what interests sociologists the most.

Symbols are so widely used that we often overlook their powerful and pervasive influence. This exercise is designed to illustrate how common and persuasive symbols can be. In addition, it takes many of us back to our childhood by reading or rereading the popular children's books about *Little Critter.*

Instructions

1. Go to your local library or neighborhood bookstore.

2. Locate the Children's section.

3. Find any *Little Critter* book written by author Mercer Mayer.

4. Read the story.

5. Write a carefully crafted essay in which you answer the questions on the worksheet.

Grading

Please check with your instructor regarding his or her grading policy. Grades or evaluations could be based on the following criteria: knowing the definition of symbols, ability to recognize society's symbols, completion of the assignment, justification of your answer, logic of your argument, and spelling and grammatical proficiency.

Reading *Little Critter*: Understanding the Power of Symbols

Worksheet

Name: _____

Please answer the following questions in a carefully constructed essay. You may use this sheet to jot down notes and ideas for the essay.

1. Is Little Critter a boy or a girl?

2. What led you to decide that Little Critter is male or female? You will notice that Litter Critter is never referred to by a personal pronoun (him/her, she/he, etc.), so there must be other factors at work.

   In formulating your answer, note the following:

   a. What clothes does Little Critter wear?

   b. With what toys does Little Critter play?

   c. In what type of activities does Little Critter engage?

   d. Is it possible that both boys and girls wear these types of clothes, play with these types of toys and do these activities? If yes, what does this say about the power and persuasiveness of symbols?

7 Crime and Deviance

Debating Deviance

Brenda L. Beagan, Dalhousie University

Rationale

This assignment includes two parts: Part I, which you will do on your own, asks you to define some key concepts. It is intended to help you focus your reading of the Deviance chapter and see where you have not fully understood something. In the next class, we will do Part II in small groups. Only students who have completed Part I will be permitted to enter a small group; thus, everyone should be equally prepared for the group work. Part II will lead toward a debate. This group work should help you construct a logical argument, forcing you to anticipate and counter opposing arguments. Building an argument will be a valuable skill for essay writing.

Instructions

1. Complete Worksheet 1, answering all questions as best you can in your own words, based on your readings about deviance and previous class discussions.

2. Next class, if Worksheet 1 is completed, you will join a small group. Introduce yourselves.

3. One person will volunteer to record notes for your group, including group members' names.

4. Complete the questions on Worksheet 2.

5. After 25 minutes, your group will be assigned a side in the debate. Pick one person to debate for you, and prepare him or her for the debate.

6. After the debate, hand in your group work plus all individual worksheets.

Grading

You should speak with your instructor regarding how the two worksheets and the whole exercise will be graded.

Debating Deviance

Worksheet 1

Name: _____

Answer the following questions in your own words based on your readings on deviance and on the previous material that we have covered in class. If this worksheet is not complete, you will not be permitted to join a small group for the next class.

What is deviance? How do you know when something is deviant?

What are social norms? How are social norms enforced in a society?

Can something be illegal yet not deviant?

Can something be deviant yet not illegal?

When does something become a crime? How?

Debating Deviance

Worksheet 2

Names:

You must have completed Worksheet 1 to participate in this group exercise. You have 25 minutes to work through the following items.

Statement: Although date rape is now a crime, it is not truly deviant because our norms and values actually support and encourage it. It does not violate social norms.

As a group, list as many points as possible that support this statement. Draw on your answers from the first worksheet.

As a group, list as many points as possible that counter (or disagree with) this statement. Draw on your answers from the first worksheet.

In an informal debate, your group will be arguing the position, "Although date rape is now a crime, it **is** truly deviant because our norms and values do not support and encourage it. It does violate social norms."

Choose one member of your group to participate in the debate on your behalf. You have 10 minutes to prepare that person.

***Identify your strongest arguments for your position. Identify the strongest arguments for the other side and how you can best counter them.

In an informal debate, your group will be arguing the position, "Although date rape is now a crime, it **is not** truly deviant because our norms and values actually support and encourage it. It does not violate social norms."

Choose one member of your group to participate in the debate on your behalf. You have 10 minutes to prepare that person.

Identify your strongest arguments for your position. Identify the strongest arguments for the other side and how you can best counter them.

Deviance Mini Case Study

Janis McCoy, Itawamba Community College

Rationale

It is important that you know and truly understand sociological theories and concepts. One of the easiest ways to demonstrate your understanding is to apply a theory or concept to a concrete example. For this activity you and your group will be writing a mini case study that will provide a concrete example of the theory (or theories) of deviance your group is assigned.

Instructions

First Day of Activity

You will be working with a group to write your case studies. You will have part of two class periods to work on your mini case study. Each group will be assigned a theory of deviance. Your group is to write a case study about the assigned theory. In this first session, your group will have about 20 minutes to discuss the theory and identify its major premises. This should also give you enough time to begin brainstorming possible ideas for your mini case study. You will have about 20 minutes in you next class to actually write your case study. Your instructor may read you a sample mini case study.

Notice:

- the mini case study is relatively short
- a fictitious person is specifically identified
- a specific situation, that could possibly be true, is described
- enough information is provided so the theory can be identified

Use Worksheet 1 as a guide for your group's discussion. One person needs to act as a recorder for your group and write down key words or phases to remind you during your next class period of what your group discussed. Your instructor will be available as your group works if you need assistance or clarification.

Before the next class period, when your group will actually write a mini case study, use Worksheet 2 to draft a mini case on your own. Bring this worksheet with you to the next class. Your instructor may collect this for a grade or credit.

Second Day of Activity

You and your group will have 20–25 minutes to write a mini case study for your assigned theory of deviance. Your instructor may read you another sample mini case study.

Use Worksheet 3 to write your case study. Be sure that all sections are completed on the worksheet and that you turn it in to your instructor before you leave class today. During your next class period we will be looking at some of the mini case studies groups have written and determining which theory is best described in each mini case.

Third Day of Activity

Today you will be applying theories of deviance to the some of the mini cases that have been written. Your instructor will provide you with a handout with several mini case studies. You will have about five minutes to read the cases and determine which theory is being described in each case study. You can write the theory in the margins. Your group will have 10–15 minutes to discuss the mini-case studies and complete Worksheet 4.

Grading

See your instructor for information on grading this exercise for your class.

Deviance Mini Case Study

Worksheet 1: Brainstorming Session

Group Members' Names:

Theory of Deviance Assigned:

Major Concepts of the Theory:

Key Components to be Included in Mini Case Study:
    About the "Person"

    About the "Situation"

Possible Ideas for Mini Case Study:

Deviance Mini Case Study

Worksheet 2: Mini Case Study Draft

Name: _____

Theory of deviance assigned to my group:

Draft for possible mini case study:

Deviance Mini Case Study

Worksheet 3: Mini Case Study

Group members:

Theory of deviance assigned:

Mini case study:

Deviance Mini Case Study

Worksheet 4: Application of Theories

Group members:

Name of person in mini case:

Theory described:

Why is this theory most applicable? (How does the case study fit this theory?) BE SPECIFIC.

Name of person in mini case:

Theory described:

Why do you feel this theory is most applicable? (How does the case study fit this theory?) BE SPECIFIC.

Images of Crime

Paul Higgins, University of South Carolina at
Columbia, and Mitchell Mackinem, Claflin University

Rationale
You will learn about and explore the common images that citizens hold about crime and criminals. Concerned observers wonder whether the taken-for-granted images that citizens hold about crime distort their view of the reality of crime. The images that people hold about crime might not adequately include the diversity of those who commit crime and the harm from their crime.

Instructions

1. Ask one or more people the following question: "When you think of crime, what specific crimes come quickly to mind?"

2. Record the responses.

3. Ask one or more people, who might or might not be the same people in Step 1, the following question: "When you think of a criminal, what picture or description of the individual comes quickly to mind? Describe that picture or description."

4. Record the responses.

5. Thank the people for their cooperation.

6. Complete the worksheet before and after class discussion.

Grading
Whether or not the exercise is graded, present your discussion of your results or the combined results of your class clearly and thoroughly. See your instructor for details on grading.

Images of Crime

Worksheet

Name: _____

1. What crimes came quickly to the minds of those who were asked? Were some crimes more frequently mentioned than other crimes by the respondents?

2. What pictures or descriptions of criminals came quickly to the minds of those who were asked? Provide the specific descriptions or a careful summary of what each person stated. If the class pools its results, did any images occur more frequently than other images? Please explain.

3. Examine your results or the combined results of your class. How would you describe the image(s) of crime that people hold? What specific crimes (or kinds of crime) are not as much a part of that image?

4. How would you summarize the image(s) of criminals that people hold? People with what kinds of characteristics are less likely to be part of that image?

5. Based on your results and responses, how well do the images of crime and the criminal held by citizens encourage them to focus on the range of crime and criminals that might harm them? Please explain.

Media Portrayals of Crime

Rebecca L. Bordt, DePauw University

Rationale

The news media have been criticized for focusing on the sensational in order to boost newspaper sales and attract viewers. In this assignment you will test the accuracy of this criticism by analyzing how one issue (crime in the United States) is portrayed in one newspaper (*The New York Times*). In the process you will learn a method of data analysis commonly used by sociologists called content analysis.

Instructions

1. Break into groups of three or four students and review the material summarized below. The general public often has an inaccurate view of crime because we rely heavily on the media for our information. The stereotypical image of crime that we are often presented by the media distorts the experience of crime in the real world and leads us to believe the following inaccurate claims:

   a. Majority of crime is "street" crime as opposed to "white collar" crime.
   b. Majority of crime is violent.
   c. Racial minority (especially African American) men commit the most crime.
   d. Crime is most often perpetrated by a stranger.
   e. The vulnerable (women, elderly, children) are most likely to be victims of crime.
   f. Most crime is solved.

2. Each group will be given a recent issue of *The New York Times* and a pair of scissors. Quickly read through the paper and cut out all news articles that have to do with crime or the criminal justice system in the United States. You can anticipate having approximately 10 articles.

3. Carefully read through each article keeping the following question in mind: In what ways is the article consistent and/or inconsistent with the stereotypic image of crime? Underline material relevant to this question. Then, record the appropriate information on the worksheet provided.

4. Next, take a step back and look at the group of articles as a whole. What conclusions would you make about crime in America based on this reading? Are these conclusions accurate or do they reinforce the stereotypical media portrayals? Explain.

5. Rejoin the rest of the class. Each group should take a turn summarizing its findings while the instructor records the summaries on the board. What patterns do you see? Are the critics right? Based on these issues of *The New York Times,* do we get a distorted image of crime?

6. Each group should hand in one completed worksheet with all the news articles attached.

Grading

Your grade will be based on the completeness and accuracy of your work. See your instructor for details.

Media Portrayals of Crime

Worksheet

Name: _____

After reading the articles, decide if the content is consistent with the stereotypic images of crime. For each article place Y (yes) or N (no) in the six columns that correspond to the stereotypic image of crime. If the article does not relate to or touch on a given stereotype, leave that box empty. Make your summary remarks below.

Article	Street Crime?	Violent?	Minority perp?	V-O strangers?	Vulnerable victim?	Crime solved?
#1						
#2						
#3						
#4						
#5						
#6						
#7						
#8						
#9						
#10						

Conclusions:

Drug Testing in the Workplace

What Would You Do?

Robert B. Pettit, Manchester College

Rationale

Even before you enrolled in this sociology course, you probably had some notions of what constitutes "deviance." Class readings and lectures may have helped you to clarify and support or revise these notions. This assignment asks you to apply your notions of deviance to a hypothetical case, and to recommend *through group discussion* how best to respond to this hypothetical case. In so doing, you may clarify further how you think about deviance, and also understand better the processes through which society defines and addresses alleged deviance.

Instructions

1. Read the following hypothetical case study:

   "Boswell and Associates is an accounting firm in a mid-size city. The firm employs over 300 people. Three months ago Chase Boswell, the firm's founder, owner, and president, convened a meeting of its management council to discuss a concern of his. He relates that he has been reading news articles about possible illegal drug use in the workplace and the employee absenteeism, loss of productivity, pilfering, embezzlement, accidents, and health costs that may be associated with it. In response to his concerns, the management council agrees to mandate a new policy of randomly testing company employees.

   "Last week, the first positive drug test (urinalysis) of the program turned up for an employee, Sonny Banks. The management council looks at Banks's file: he is 28 years old, unmarried, in his third year at the firm, with job performance ratings above the 80th percentile (a very good rating at the firm).

   "Boswell calls Banks in and confronts him with the positive test results. Banks denies using illegal drugs. Boswell says he'll give him the chance to take an immediate re-test. Banks refuses, saying that he's read that such tests may be only 95% accurate, and if it was wrong the first time, why trust his fate to it again? Boswell then asks Banks to take a lie detector test; Banks refuses that as well. Boswell reminds Banks that mandatory drug testing is now company policy; Banks says he had no voice in formulating the policy and in fact disagrees with it. Boswell says that Banks must take the drug test now and pass it or immediately submit himself to a drug rehabilitation program. If he refuses to do either, he will be considered to be guilty of illegal drug use and/or insubordination, in which case company policy dictates that he be fired. Banks points to his strong performance ratings at the firm and the absence of any prior disciplinary concerns; he demands that the matter be dropped without prejudice."

2. Now, having read this scenario, *what do you think should happen next? Who's right and who's wrong here? What should be done to address this situation?* Use the worksheet provided on the next page to write down your thoughts and your recommendations. Your course instructor will divide your class into groups to discuss this matter in class. Your task as a group will be to make recommendations about what should happen next. As a group, decide: *Who's right and who's wrong here? What should be done to address this situation?* If you believe you do not have enough information on certain points, couch your recommendations in terms of, "If *X* is the case, then we recommend that. . . ." Try to achieve a group consensus with which every group member can agree in part, if not in full. Appoint a group recorder who will write down your group's three or four main recommendations, with a brief explanation and justification for each. Include direct quotations or paraphrases from individual group members to give specificity and concreteness to your group's general conclusions. Your group recorder will announce these recommendations to the class when asked to do so by your instructor.

Grading

Your instructor may or may not choose to make this a graded exercise. If grades are to be assigned for this exercise, you will likely be evaluated on criteria such as these:

- whether or not *all* members of your group are actively involved in discussing the issues and working toward consensus
- whether or not your group members are able to stay on task and refrain from extraneous discussion topics
- whether or not your recommendations are clearly stated and thoughtfully justified
- whether or not you are able to exercise a *sociological perspective* in your discussions

Because this is a group exercise, you will be evaluated *as a group* and not individually.

Drug Testing in the Workplace: What Would You Do?

Worksheet

Name: _____

Once you have read the "Boswell/Banks" scenario on the previous page, use this page to write down your thoughts on the following questions. Your comments here will be the basis of your contribution to your in-class group discussion.

1. What are your recommendations regarding what should happen next to address this impasse between Boswell and Banks?

2. Who do you think is right and who do you think is wrong in this scenario?

3. What should be done to address this situation?

8 Social Institutions

Housework

Division of Labor

Judy Aulette, University of
North Carolina at Charlotte

Rationale

You have heard a lecture and read about how housework is divided in families. The sociological literature shows that housework is a problem in many households, because it is not divided equally or fairly. Often, women do most of the housework—even if they are in the paid labor force as well. This assignment has you think personally about what such a household should do (if anything) to change this situation. You will also place your thoughts in the context of a theoretical approach within sociology.

Instructions

1. Listen to a lecture and read the material about how housework is divided in families.

2. Write a response to the first item on the worksheet individually.

3. Listen to a lecture on the theoretical models that try to explain why housework is divided unequally.

4. Get into groups, read all of the paragraphs written by your group members, and try to decide which theoretical model best fits each.

5. Provide a short quote from your paragraph that provides evidence for the decision regarding your paragraph.

Grading

See your instructor for details about how this assignment will be graded.

Housework: Division of Labor

Worksheet

Name: _____

Imagine that you are a heterosexual in a household with a spouse. The woman is doing more than half of the housework. Write a paragraph explaining what you think needs to be done to address this inequity.

After listening to the lecture on the theoretical models that try to explain why housework is divided unequally, get into groups with two or three other students. Read all of the paragraphs that your group members wrote and decide into which theoretical model each best fits. Write the name of the theoretical model that your group decided your paragraph fits best.

Provide a short quote from the paragraph that provides evidence for your decision.

Parenthood

Defining Family

Judy Aulette, University of
North Carolina at Charlotte

Rationale

Child custody cases present difficult challenges. Deciding who should raise a child makes us question our ideas about what being a real parent is. Social factors such as the time, care, and physical support that adults give to children are critical issues. Biology has also played an important role in our deliberations about custody. But even biology can be confusing with the development of new technologies that enable eggs and sperm to be stored, eggs to be fertilized outside the human body, and women who are not the egg donor to carry the pregnancy to term and deliver the baby. Furthermore, the biological relationship between a mother and baby and a father and baby is different. Males and females contribute similar genetic material, but females also endure the pregnancy and deliver the baby. This assignment, therefore, is designed to make you think about what a "real parent" is and how we can best decide who should raise a child when there are competing parties.

Instructions

Listen to the lecture and/or do the reading on Baby M. Imagine that you are the judge in the case. To whom would you award the child? Would you give the child to Mary Beth Whitehead, to Bill and Betsy Stern, or to someone else? Write your answers on the worksheet explaining what your decision would be and why you reached that judgment. What are the most important facts in the case?

Grading

See your instructor for details concerning how this assignment will be graded.

Parenthood: Defining Family

Worksheet

Name: _____

To whom would you award Baby M?

On what basis did you reach that decision?

What are the most important factors in the case?

Family History Project

Mark R. Warren, Harvard University

Rationale

In this course, we are discussing sociology as a way to understand the intersection between biography and history, between self and society. In this project you will sketch a history of your family, focusing on a number of issues that we are discussing in the course. You will be asked to consider the influences of your family, societal structures, and your own individual choices on your life history. By interviewing family members, you will have the chance to do a piece of sociological research. We will devote time in class to the discussion of your findings with each other. These discussions will give us the opportunity to consider how the larger social trends we discuss in this course are mirrored in the history of our families.

Instructions

1. Interview six family members, going as far back in generations as possible. Face-to-face interviews are better; but some of you may have to conduct interviews over the telephone. Please draw upon any other sources of information (photos, diaries, videos) that are useful. The questions on the attached worksheet can be used as a suggested framework for your interviews.

2. On the basis of the interviews, write a 7–8 page essay. At the end of the essay include a list of the family members interviewed and any materials examined. You may attach photographs, if you'd like.

3. Be prepared to share the results of your investigation with other class members. In that context, you are free to withhold any information that is sensitive, confidential, or that otherwise makes you uncomfortable. In addition, I would like to insist that all class members treat the experiences of all of our families with the respect they deserve. Our goal is not to pass judgment on each other. The purpose of this project is self-understanding and greater understanding of the commonality and differences of social experience in the United States.

Grading

See your instructor for information on the grading of this exercise.

Family History Project

Worksheet

Name: _____

    The following are questions you might like to address in your interviews and in the essay. You may use this sheet to jot down your ideas.

1. How did your family come to be in the United States (for immigrants)? Why did they come?

2. What has been your family's work experience here in the United States?

   How have the jobs held by family members changed through the generations?

   Has your family's standard of living improved, gotten worse, or experienced some combination of the two over time? Why?

3. How has the family structure and the roles of men and women changed?

   Has your family become closer (personally and/or geographically) or more dispersed?

4. What has been your family's experience with racism, prejudice, or oppression?

5. What kind of participation has your family had in social, cultural, and political organizations—or in efforts to create societal change?

6. What has been your family's experience with the educational system?

7. How have religious practices changed over time?

Rather than answering these questions mechanically point by point, try to develop themes in your essay, telling good stories. You may therefore focus more on some questions rather than others. In addition, please include any other important experiences that have shaped your family's development, but are not captured by one of these questions.

The following are questions for your reflection, but you may ask family members for their views on these questions too. Please incorporate your thoughts on these questions into the essay.

8. Do you think your family experiences have been typical of other Americans, or unusual?

9. To what extent have your family's experiences been the result of social structural forces, of accidental factors, and/or of choices and decisions made by its members?

The last part of your essay should answer the following question:

10. To what extent do you think you are a product of your family's history? To what extent has your life been influenced by the broader social forces of American society and by your own choices?

Tommy's Story

Marjorie Altergott, DePaul University

Rationale

This exercise will facilitate cooperative exploration of and learning about the context of health.

Instructions

1. Individually complete Part I of the worksheet by writing your definition of health.

2. Read or listen to "Tommy's Story." (Your instructor will provide it for you.)

3. As a group, carry out each step of the exercise as explained by the facilitator/your instructor.

4. Individually, write a reflective response, probably about one page in length, to the question posed by your facilitator/instructor for Part II of the worksheet.

Grading

See your instructor for details about grading this exercise for your class. Grading is usually based on the quality and development of your reflective writing for Part II of the worksheet. Criteria are as follows:

Well developed: Your introduction states a clear, relevant, main point. This is adequately supported by explaining several sub-points which include sufficient detail and/or examples to communicate your thoughts effectively. You complete your response with a statement that summarizes your supporting points and how they are related to your main point.

Partly developed: Your introduction states a clear, relevant, main point, but the number of sub-points is inadequate to support it strongly, or they require more detail or examples to adequately communicate your thoughts. Or, your main point is not clear, although there are several points you make, at least some that are well communicated through detail and/or examples, which seem to be related to an overall major theme. Your concluding statement may be missing, or it does not summarize the main idea or relationships among sub-points.

Poorly developed: Your main point is not relevant to the topic or is not clearly stated. The information in the writing is disconnected and it is not clear what main point it could be referring to. Your concluding statement is missing or is unclear.

Tommy's Story

Worksheet

Name: _____

    A. How do you define health?

    B. Write a reflective response to the question posed by your facilitator. Begin your response with an introduction stating a clear, relevant main point or generalization. Support your main point with several related ideas or sub-points, using sufficient detail and specific examples to communicate your ideas clearly. Conclude with a summarizing statement that points out the connection between your supporting points and their connection to your main point (use the back of this page if needed).

Mapping Census Data for Your Town

Julie A. Pelton, Illinois Wesleyan University, and
Frank D. Beck, Illinois State University

Rationale

Communities play an important role in our lives. Some would say their role in shaping us is second in importance only to our families. The places we have lived serve as the nexus of a number of social forces affecting who we have become (i.e., the economy, environment, culture, education, etc.). It is also true that all places are not the same; they are structured differently and these structures have changed over time. You are now going to have the chance to look at how socioeconomic characteristics are distributed within your town and to write why you think they're distributed that way. The intent is for you to see your town differently than you've ever seen it before and for you to come up with reasons for why the statistics are the way they are and why the maps look the way they do.

For this assignment you will need to pick a town in the United States on which you want to focus. You will need to know something about this place—where it is, what its geography is like, what county it is in, and where the town is in the county (an atlas will help you with the last two points). It is best, therefore, if you focus on the town you grew up in or the place you now call home. Using the instructions from class and those in the "Specific Instructions" below for working with the American Fact Finder (Census) web page (http://factfinder.census.gov), you will map the distribution of various socioeconomic characteristics of your town or city.

Instructions

1. First, you will map the distribution of six census variables for your town. Three of the variables should be:

   a. Median value of specified owner-occupied housing
   b. Percentage of families below the poverty level
   c. Percentage of housing units built before 1940

   These variables (the census website calls them "themes") are not listed in alphabetical order but can be organized by subject area for easier searching.

2. You will then need to pick three more variables you want to map and write about. You should stick with the variables that are already in percentage (race/ethnicity, education, % persons below 50% of poverty) or average/median form (income, housing values, gross rent, etc.). A variable that is simply a count of persons in a certain category will vary more by the number of residents in the space than by socioeconomic differences. Obtain the minimum and maximum for your chosen variables as well.

3. After mapping each of these six variables, describe what the maps look like using your knowledge of neighborhoods and streets. The legend next to the map will tell you the lowest (minimum) and highest (maximum) possible values for that variable in that place. Record these values on your worksheet.

4. You will print out and turn in all six maps. Indicate on the printed maps where you live(d) in the neighborhood or town and number or title each map to match the label you gave them on the worksheet.

5. Write a description for each map on the worksheets provided, and staple them together with the maps. In the description, you should answer the following questions:

   a. How is the variable distributed? What does the shading mean to you? Why is the variable distributed this way for your town or neighborhood? Why is it distributed this way for areas around your home or your town?

   b. If there are any drastic differences within your map (e.g., shading changes abruptly where a street or some railroad tracks are), you should mention these. Of course, the fact that there are no major differences within your area may be noteworthy as well.

   c. Lastly, do these maps tell you anything about your town that you did not know before or do they reinforce what you already knew?

   d. What about the structure of your town explains all the maps as a whole? Picture the maps overlapping each other; what patterns do you see across the maps?

The descriptions in your write-up should not be simplistic. Reporting a 0–2% poverty rate isn't enough and cannot be explained by the fact that your town is middle class; you should describe why you think your town is middle class and able to keep poverty low (refer to the attached sample worksheet describing the distribution of poverty in Bloomington-Normal, IL).

Grading

See your instructor for details on grading this exercise. Usually, your grade is based primarily on how well you describe the maps. You should assume that your instructor knows very little about your town or neighborhood and so you should explain in detail why the variable in question is distributed the way it is. This includes listing and discussing the minimum and maximum values for the place you are describing.

Specific Instructions for How to Use the American Fact Finder Web Page

To Begin:

1. In your browser go to http://factfinder.census.gov.

2. Click on the button to the left marked "DataSets" and select "Decennial Census" from the menu.

3. Choose "2000 Summary File 3 (SF 3)—Sample Data."

4. Click on "Thematic Maps" to the right.

5. To the right of "Select Geographic Type" click the down arrow and choose "Place."

6. To right of "Select a State" click the down arrow and choose one.

7. Underneath "Select a geographic area" pick a town for which you wish to map data. Then click "Next."

8. Underneath "Select a theme" scroll down and pick a variable (remember that three of these are required; you pick three others). If you wish, you can choose to organize themes "by subject" rather than using the "show all themes" option. Themes will then be grouped together, which may make it easier to find specific variables.

9. To the right of the list of variables is a blue button called "Show Map." Click it. A map for your town, showing the distribution of data, will pop up.

Now you have choices:

10. You can reposition the map by zooming in or out or by using the blue arrows to the outside of the map to move north, south, east, or west. You may wish to reposition the map based on your address, using the menu on the left-hand side of the screen. It will automatically zoom in to your address and then you'll have to zoom out to talk about your neighborhood in relation to others around it and in the city.

11. It is your job to position the map in such a way that you can indicate where you live (by placing a star on the printed copies) and yet you can show variation or lack of variation across the city. Zooming in will lead to street names that will help you identify the location you want.

12. At the top of the map is a pull-down window that says "census tract." To get more detail in your map, showing more variation across neighborhoods, you can change that to "block groups." The map will be redrawn. For those from cities of 1 million or more people, census tracts are detailed enough. If you change between tracts and block groups, you'll have to reposition the map again.

Printing and Saving:

Once you're comfortable with the way the map looks (zooming in/out or centered the way you want), print it by using the "Print/Download" menu at the top of the web page. Some of you may want to save your maps to a disk and print them somewhere else. To do so:

—right click on map and select "save image as . . ." from the menu

—select the directory you want to save the map to and change the name to something you can remember/find (e.g., poverty map)

—to save the legend, do the same as you did for the map, but give it a different name (e.g., poverty legend)

—open the map and legend from the directory in which you saved them (Microsoft Photo Editor opens .gif files). When windows for the map and legend are both open, you can copy the legend and paste it into the map.

Definitions You Need to Know for this Assignment:

Places: towns that are incorporated or designated as so by the U.S. Census (a Bureau within the U.S. Department of Commerce)

Census Tract: a census defined space that consists of approximately 4,000 persons

Block Group: a census defined space that consists of approximately 1,000–1,300 persons; there are 3–4 block groups in a census tract

Mapping Census Data for Your Town

Sample Worksheet

What town and county did you map? _____ Normal, IL: Mclean County _____

Map #1: _____ Percentage of Families That Are Poor _____

Description: Minimum: __0__ Maximum: __90__

Most of Normal has a relatively low percent poor; between 0 and 13.3 percentage. However, there are areas of considerably higher poverty. There are several areas that are between 34.7 and 50 percent poor. Based on my knowledge of the city, the darker squares on the northern side (Normal) of the city are a surprise. I thought that Normal had less concentrated poverty than that. However, there are several mobile home parks and low-income housing units in the general area of the dark squares on the top left of this map. The highest poverty (~100%) sits just south of Illinois State University. I am unsure why there's such high poverty there. Students don't count as families, so they would not be included on this map. It is also interesting that the rural areas of the county have such low percentge poor. I used to think that farmers might be less well off than city dwellers. While there are certainly some areas that have highly concentrated poverty, the county as a whole is not extremely poor. Bloomington-Normal is a growing town with mostly white-collar jobs, a strong economy, and a very low unemployment rate: all accounting for the fairly low levels of poverty.

Mapping Census Data for Your Town

Worksheet

Name: _____

What town and county did you map? _____

Map #1: _____

Description: Minimum: _____   Maximum: _____

Your Name: _____

What town and county did you map? _____

Map #2: _____

Description: Minimum: _____   Maximum: _____

Your Name: _____

What town and county did you map? _____

Map #3: _____

Description: Minimum: _____   Maximum: _____

Your Name: _____

What town and county did you map? _____

Map #4: _____

Description: Minimum: _____   Maximum: _____

Your Name: _____

What town and county did you map? _____

Map #5: _____

Description: Minimum: _____   Maximum: _____

Your Name: _____

What town and county did you map? _____

Map #6: _____

Description: Minimum: _____   Maximum: _____

9 Multi-Topic Exercises

Song Analysis Project

Mellisa Holtzman, Ball State University

Rationale

Music, as many of you realize, is so much more than mere entertainment. It provides a commentary on many aspects of life, both good and bad. It helps people relate to situations that they have faced or better understand those that they have not yet faced. It stirs a variety of emotions while simultaneously providing people with an emotional outlet. In short, music makes a statement about life while also impacting it.

What, then, does music have to do with a sociology course? The answer is "Quite a bit." Because music so often reflects what happens in our world, it can be a particularly useful learning tool. Thus, this exercise is designed to demonstrate, through music, the usefulness of the concepts that you have been learning about in class. In short, it provides you with an opportunity to *apply* what you have been learning to music. This process will help clarify class concepts for you and make any misunderstandings apparent. Likewise, it will demonstrate the usefulness of class material, because you will be able to see it in action (so to speak). Finally, this project is also designed to give you practice for any larger song analysis projects that your instructor might require.

Instructions

1. Get into your pre-assigned groups and listen to the song being played for the class.

2. Using the lyrics that are on display, you must determine as a group which class concept(s) the song relates to and why.

3. Pick out specific lyrics from the song that are especially useful in demonstrating this song's relationship to class materials.

4. Pick one group member to be the recorder. This person should list all group members' names and group answers on the worksheet.

5. Using the worksheet, write out the song analysis that you began to construct during Steps 2 and 3. It is important that you save the writing for last so that the analysis you turn in is well thought out,

organized, and well written. It might be helpful to use scratch paper while working through Steps 2 and 3.

6. Try to finish this project within 15 minutes and be prepared to discuss your analysis with the class at the end of that time.

7. Turn in the group's worksheet at the end of class (only one worksheet per group needs to be turned in).

Grading

See your instructor for details about grading. Generally, each analysis will be graded on organization and the insight of the group analysis. This grading does not mean that every possible avenue of analysis must be explored in order to receive full credit, but it does mean that thoughtful connections between class material and the song should be apparent in the group's write-up.

Song Analysis Project

Worksheet

Names of group members present:

This worksheet is designed to help you develop and organize your analysis. The Roman numerals below roughly correspond to sections of a paper (introduction, body, and conclusion).

I. Introduction
In this section, write a brief paragraph that tells the reader (in other words, the instructor) which song is being analyzed and to which sociological topics it relates. Remember, this section is the introduction—it sets up the rest of the paper.

II. Analysis
This section is the heart of the paper. Explain in detail which concepts are exemplified in this song and why. Be sure to fully *define/describe* each of the concepts as well as demonstrate their relation to the song via quoted lyrics. Use the back of this worksheet or attach a separate sheet of paper.

III. Conclusion

    Provide a brief summary of the analysis.

"All of A Sudden . . ."

Exploring Sociology in Everyday Life

Sarah E. Rusche and Kris Macomber,
North Carolina State University

Rationale

The major goal of this assignment is to encourage you to develop the socio-logical perspective and use it to examine your "ordinary" everyday lives. In doing so, you will be able to see the broader patterns organizing your own experiences. Rather than studying sociology as just another college "subject," the learning objective here is that you work as *apprentices* of sociology. To successfully do this, you must draw on sociological concepts and theories in your analyses and ultimately "do sociology." This assignment gives you the opportunity to use sociology to make sense of your everyday life.

Instructions

1. This assignment requires you to observe your everyday experiences through a sociological lens.

2. You must use what you have learned about sociology to interpret your experiences and develop an analysis of what you observe.

3. This assignment does not require you to go somewhere special to make these observations. In fact, the point is to pay closer attention to the *ordinary* experiences of your everyday life. Some examples include: eating at a campus dining hall, watching television or movies, listening to music, grocery shopping, reading a magazine, playing a game, attending a party, talking to your parents, having a family dinner over the holidays, and so forth.

4. Remember that sociology is everywhere!

5. Using the "stem" (sentence starter) below, write an essay describing the experience you observed using the sociological perspective (including relevant course material) to make sense of your social

environment. This phrase must be included at the beginning of your essay:

"All of a sudden, I found myself thinking sociologically when I . . ."

6. You will complete this assignment three times throughout the semester using three *different* observations.

7. You will complete the *first* essay (1–2 pages) early in the semester when your sociological skills are limited. This essay will not be graded, but is required. Think of the first essay as a practice round. You will get critical feedback to improve the second essay.

8. The *second* essay (2–3 pages) will be done about halfway through the semester. By then you will have acquired a fair number of analytical tools and will be able to provide a complex sociological analysis of the event, activity, or experience observed. Remember, you must use course material to guide and interpret what you observe.

9. Finally, the *third* essay (3–4 pages) you will write at the very end of the semester. This last essay should show your growth from a fledgling sociologist to a sociologically sophisticated thinker.

10. Remember to draw on important concepts and theories and make these ideas come to life in your analyses.

Grading

Please see your instructor for information on grading this exercise for your course.

"All of A Sudden . . ." Exploring Sociology in Everyday Life

Worksheet

Name: _____

Essay #1

Use this worksheet as a guide for your observations and to jot down some notes. These questions are designed so that you can go out into your social world and find the answers through sociological observation. Some questions are more or less applicable to some situations than others, depending on your observation. Use your best judgment when deciding which questions make sense to ask in your situation.

1. Initial Observations

   Describe the observation site/situation:

   - Where are you?

   - Who is there and how many?

   - What general activity is taking place?

2. Sociological Observations

   Describe the sociological context:

   - Are you involved in the situation actively or as a mere observer?

   - To what social groups do the people belong (consider race, gender, age, etc.)?

   - Who is doing what with whom or to whom?

   - Why are the people here (by choice, by need, by force, etc.)?

   - What do you see going on here *sociologically*?

- How are people interacting with one another?

- How are people reacting to one another?

3. Sociological Analysis

   Analyze/Interpret the observations from above:

   - Which course materials can be used to make sense of these observations?

   - Which course readings support or refute these observations?

   - Which course concepts, theories, films, discussions, and so on, apply to these observations and guide your interpretation? How so?

   - How can you relate this specific experience to larger patterns of interaction?

   - What questions need to be asked to deepen your interpretation?

"All of A Sudden . . ." Exploring Sociology in Everyday Life

Worksheet

Name: _____

Essay #2

Use this worksheet as a guide for your observations and to jot down some notes. These questions are designed so that you can go out into your social world and find the answers through sociological observation. Some questions are more or less applicable to some situations than others, depending on your observation. Use your best judgment when deciding which questions make sense to ask in your situation.

1. Initial Observations

   Describe the observation site/situation:

   - Where are you?

   - Who is there and how many?

   - What general activity is taking place?

2. Sociological Observations

   Describe the sociological context:

   - Are you involved in the situation actively or as a mere observer?

   - To what social groups do the people belong? (consider race, gender, age, etc.)

   - Who is doing what with whom or to whom?

   - Why are the people here (by choice, by need, by force, etc.)?

- What do you see going on here *sociologically*?

- How are people interacting with one another?

- How are people reacting to one another?

3. Sociological Analysis

   Analyze/Interpret the observations from above:

   - Which course materials can be used to make sense of these observations?

   - Which course readings support or refute these observations?

   - Which course concepts, theories, films, discussions, and so on. apply to these observations and guide your interpretation? How so?

   - How can you relate this specific experience to larger patterns of interaction?

   - What questions need to be asked to deepen your interpretation?

"All of A Sudden . . ." Exploring Sociology in Everyday Life

Worksheet

Name: _____

Essay #3

Use this worksheet as a guide for your observations and to jot down some notes. These questions are designed so that you can go out into your social world and find the answers through sociological observation. Some questions are more or less applicable to some situations than others, depending on your observation. Use your best judgment when deciding which questions make sense to ask in your situation.

1. Initial Observations

   Describe the observation site/situation:

   - Where are you?

   - Who is there and how many?

   - What general activity is taking place?

2. Sociological Observations

   Describe the sociological context:

   - Are you involved in the situation actively or as a mere observer?

   - To what social groups do the people belong (consider race, gender, age, etc.)?

   - Who is doing what with whom or to whom?

   - Why are the people here (by choice, by need, by force, etc.)?

   - What do I see going on here *sociologically*?

- How are people interacting with one another?

- How are people reacting to one another?

3. Sociological Analysis

   Analyze/Interpret the observations from above:

   - Which course materials can be used to make sense of these observations?

   - Which course readings support or refute these observations?

   - Which course concepts, theories, films, discussions, etc., apply to these observations and guide your interpretation? How so?

   - How can you relate this specific experience to larger patterns of interaction?

   - What questions need to be asked to deepen your interpretation?

Critical Reports on Contemporary Social Problems

John J. Shalanski, Luzerne County
Community College

Rationale

The purpose of this assignment is to help you define and understand what constitutes a social problem. By reading about the problems that you consider important, you develop a better awareness of your social world. You can choose a problem in your local community, in the nation, or a more global issue that affects everyone. Writing critically about the problem you select and attempting to develop solutions will help clarify your own perspective and values. You will be able to look at how the problem originated and examine what can be done about it.

Instructions

1. Read an article on a current social problem from a daily newspaper (local or national) or a weekly news magazine (such as *Time, Newsweek, U.S. News and World Report,* etc.). It does not have to be a problem that we discussed in class, but it should be an issue about which you are concerned.

2. Cut out the article (or copy it) and attach it to a paper on which you have addressed all of the following questions:
   - Why is this problem considered a "social problem"?
   - When, how, and where did the problem originate?
   - What other social problems are related to this problem?
   - What groups are affected by it?
   - Who benefits (or stands to gain) from the problem?
   - Who is hurt by it?
   - How does it affect you personally?
   - What can be done, and by whom, to alleviate the problem?

3. Your report should be clear, brief, and concise (no longer than two typewritten pages). You can list the questions and answer them, or organize the report in a narrative form.

Grading
▬▬▬▬

You will be graded on your understanding of the social problem, your critical analysis of it based on the instructions, and your ability to communicate your thoughts in writing. If you have any questions on whether a certain issue constitutes a social problem, please see the instructor.

Critical Reports on Contemporary Social Problems

Worksheet

Name: _____

A social problem is a condition that threatens the quality of life for people in a society and their most cherished values. It is a condition that a significant number of people believe should be remedied through collective action.[1] Answer the following questions in your paper; you can use this space to brainstorm your answers.

- Why is this problem considered a social problem?

- When, how, and where did this problem originate? Has it been around a while? Are we just seeing it publicized more?

- What other social problems are related to this one? List all of the social problems that are related to the problem that you chose—both as a cause of it and as an effect of it.

- What groups are affected by this problem?

- Who is hurt by it? Is anyone immune?

- Think critically: Who benefits (or stands to gain) from this problem?

- How does it affect you personally? Think about your own life and how this problem intersects with it. Address this question even if you have never encountered the problem personally.

- What can be done, and by whom, to alleviate the problem? Address all possible solutions that you can think of. Most experts might be baffled, so do not be afraid to use your imagination and to list whatever you think will work. (Use separate sheet of paper and attach it to this worksheet.)

Note

1. Kornblum, William & Julian, Joseph (1998). *Social Problems* (9th ed.). Upper Saddle River, NJ: Prentice Hall.

Literary and Artistic Reflections on War, Terror, and Violence

Danielle Taana Smith, Rochester Institute of Technology

Rationale

On September 11, 2001, the Twin Towers of the World Trade Center were bombed, creating havoc not just in New York and the United States, but in the world at large. Daily we watch on television as the death toll escalates for American soldiers in Iraq, and the death toll is a hundredfold greater for Iraqis, a reality that is a sideline on the news. On April 16, 2007, we were horrified by the senseless killings on the campus of Virginia Tech. These events and others mandate that classrooms offer students strategies for grappling with the realities of war, terror, and violence, at both a personal and intimate level, but also on a larger and more global scale. This exercise allows you to evaluate these contemporary realities and has been integrated into introductory sociology and anthropology courses.

This assignment is a semester-long exercise. It begins with individual reflection and expression, and then progresses to sharing these ideas with your classmates both in groups and with the class as a whole. The learning objective is to provide an opportunity for you to research the issues of war, terror, and violence and to develop your own ideas based on your research. These ideas will be expressed through writing and art. You will present and discuss your ideas with your classmates in small groups, noting how and why you share similar or dissimilar ideas. You will also present ideas emerging out of group discussions to the entire class.

Individual literary and artistic works may be submitted to the *War and Terror: Curricular Strategies* website to be shared with a larger audience. Website link: http://www.rit.edu/cla/sociology/warterror/index.html

Instructions

1. To gain a better understanding of factors that contribute to war, terror, and/or violence, and of the people around the world and in our communities who experience these conditions, read an autobiography,

essay, ethnography, or historical or personal account that relates to any of these issues.

2. Critique your reading in a reaction paper (2 pages). Discuss how this reading showed a human dimension of the experience of war, terror, and/or violence. Discuss the impact of the reading on you: Did it provide you with any new insight? Did it make you change any of your ideological positions?

3. Write an essay (5 pages) or create a work of visual art that conveys your own ideas about war, terror, and/or violence. If you select writing an essay, the essay must include an introduction, review of previous literature on your theme, a discussion of your ideas, a concluding section, and a bibliography. If you select creating a work of art, provide a briefer essay (2 pages) that describes your work.

4. After comments from the instructor, revise and electronically resubmit your work for inclusion in the final collection of essays and art.

5. Orally present your work to the class (5 to 10 minute presentations).

Grading

See your instructor for information on grading this exercise in your course.

Literary and Artistic Reflections
on War, Terror, and Violence

Worksheet: Reaction paper

Name: _____

1. Summarize the reading. What is the author's story?

2. Select one idea or event from the reading and discuss its significance for you personally.

3. How can the author's experiences be used to examine war, terror, and violence on a larger scale?

4. How has reflective learning and applying your knowledge through writing and art enhanced your classroom learning?

Literary and Artistic Reflections on War, Terror, and Violence

Worksheet: Essay or Work of Art

Name: _____

1. Select one of the three general topical areas (war, terror, violence) as a focus.

2. Refine your focus. For example, if you selected terror, what specific issue about terror do you intend to examine?

3. Provide your motivation for selecting this issue.

4. In what ways has reflective learning and applying your knowledge through writing and art enhanced your classroom learning?

10 Course Structure and Process

Student Empowerment

Student-Designed Syllabus

Ada Haynes, Tennessee Technological University

Rationale

Student empowerment is a growing trend in academia. Studies show that student empowerment is related to motivation, participation, and problem-solving skills. Research similarly shows that when students are interested and motivated, they learn more. In this class, you are going to have a unique opportunity. You are going to participate in the selection of course goals, objectives, and requirements. In short, you are going to work together with your professor to design the course syllabus. You will be using the consensus model of decision making. Using this model, everyone must agree on each step. Although this process might be more time consuming than simply voting, it assures us that everyone is committed to the goals and success of this course. This course should be a true partnership between you, the students, and your professor.

Instructions

1. The first step in designing a syllabus for a course is to explore what it is that you want to gain from a course. Complete Part I of your worksheet. You should describe in detail why you signed up for this course. You should be very specific what you would like to learn in this course. If you are not sure about what you might learn about in this course, open your text. Look at the table of contents. Flip through the chapters. Note areas that are particularly interesting to you. If you are not sure whether a particular area could be included in the course, ask your professor.

2. The second step in designing a syllabus is to combine both your goals and the goals and objectives of your instructor. Read the goals and objectives given to you by your professor.

3. Consider how you like to be evaluated in courses. How should your professor fairly and accurately evaluate whether you have accomplished your learning goals and the professor's goals? Complete Part II of your worksheet. Begin by including any mandated requirements given to you by your professor.

4. As a class, discuss the course requirements that each person developed. Remember that consensus is necessary. You should be prepared to compromise. Also, remember that the instructor can always revert to traditional methods of developing a course syllabus.

5. Now that the class has developed a list of course requirements, it is time to allocate a percentage to each of those requirements. Copy the list of requirements developed by the class and assign each requirement a percentage.

6. As a class, discuss the different percentage distribution for the requirements that each individual developed. Reach a consensus as to the percentage allocated for each requirement. Make sure that the percentage fully reflects the course goals and objectives and the amount of effort needed to fulfill the requirement.

Grading

See your instructor for details regarding how this exercise will be graded. Remember that even if you are not assigned an official grade for this exercise, it might ultimately affect your grade more than any other activity throughout the semester because it will determine the course requirements and how your grade will be computed. Therefore your grades for this course are directly dependent upon your input into this exercise.

Student Empowerment: Student-Designed Syllabus

Worksheet

Name: _____

Part I: Goals and Objectives:

    1. Why are you taking this course?

    2. What do you hope to learn from this course?

Part II: Course Requirements

    Below please list the criteria upon which you would like to be evaluated in this course. Make sure that they are appropriate measures of your learning and correspond to the objectives for this class. Some examples of appropriate criteria include sociological research project, exams, quizzes, class attendance and participation, documentary, journals, projects, debates, leading class for a day, and reaction papers. You may also be creative and develop additional criteria of your own.

    1.

    2.

    3.

    4.

    5.

    6.

7.

8.

Part III: Percentage Points Allocated for Each Course Requirement
Now that the class has agreed upon the course requirements, you should assign a percentage to each of the course requirements.

1.

2.

3.

4.

5.

6.

7.

8.

Write here your reflections on what you have learned from completing this exercise.

MyPage

Student Information

Janis McCoy, Itawamba Community College

Rationale   It is very important for me, as your instructor, to learn your names as quickly as possible. This activity will enable me to do that. One of the things that helps me learn who you are is to associate you with something specific about you. MyPage is designed for you to provide me with a picture of yourself and information that I can associate with you. This activity will give you the opportunity to share some of your experiences, achievements, and goals. These will be valuable in helping me learn about you as quickly as possible. I hope this will also help you as you learn sociology by thinking about your personal experiences in relation to various topics we will cover in Introduction to Sociology this semester.

Instructions   You will have about a week to think about and work on this first and very important assignment. MyPage should be no longer than one typed 8 ½ × 11 page of regular white paper. Be as creative as possible in developing and presenting your page. Your page should include

- A picture of yourself—it may be a still shot or an action shot, preferably scanned onto your page
- 2–3 paragraphs with the following **personal information**:
  o family background
  o places you have lived or visited
  o achievements
  o hobbies/interests
  o other life experiences
- 1–2 paragraphs with the following **student information**:
  o college activities in which you participate, if any
  o why you are taking this course (for many of you it may be that this class is simply required in your major field of study, but you could describe why you are interested in that general field)
  o what you hope to learn

- 1–2 paragraphs about **your lifetime goals**, such as:
  - what you hope to accomplish in life
  - major field of study and where you hope it will take you (if you are undecided, that's okay, but think about areas you are considering and why)
  - how you think sociology can help you attain your educational and lifetime goals

Each section of your page should be clearly distinguishable. You may do that by using different colors of type (yellow print should not be used, because it is very difficult to read on white paper), different fonts, placement of information on your page, and so on.

Grading

See you instructor for information on grading this exercise in your course.

The next pages provide you with a worksheet and sample layout to help you develop your page. The sample is just that—a sample—there are many creative ways for you to present your information.

MyPage: Student Information

Preparation and Brainstorming Worksheet

Name: _____

Title:

How will I include my name in the title?

How will I display the title of my page?

   Font?

   Color?

   Other?

Picture:

   What type picture of myself will I use?

   Where will I get my picture (access student ID photo, scan or download another photo)?

   How will I get it on MyPage?

   Will I need someone to help me get it onto MyPage? If so, who can help me?

Personal Information:

   Family background to be included:

   Places I've lived:

   Places I've visited:

Achievements:

    Honors, recognitions, I have received:

    Things I have done I regard as major events in my life:

    Hobbies/interests I have:

    Other experiences:

Student Information:

    College activities in which I participate (sports, band, chorus):

    College clubs to which I belong:

    Why I am taking this sociology course:

Lifetime goals:

    What I hope to accomplish in my lifetime:

    Career I plan, at this point in time, to pursue:

    How I feel sociology will help me attain my lifetime goals:

Joe Student's Page
(Sample)

Personal Information

Family background

Places I have lived or visited

Achievements

Hobbies/interest

Other life experiences

Student Information

College activities in which I participate, if any

Why am I taking this course

What I hope to learn

Lifetime Goals

What I hope to accomplish in life

Major field of study (if undecided, what areas am I considering)

How I think sociology can help me attain my educational and lifetime goals

Initial Group Assessment

John R. Bowman, University
of North Carolina at Pembroke

Rationale

All groups develop and modify rules of behavior (norms) that are appropriate for membership in that group. Effective groups have members who are willing to periodically evaluate themselves and change in ways that contribute to being an even more effective group. Both leaders and members contribute to this ongoing process. This exercise is designed for you as an individual to assess your group's effectiveness, and it should be utilized periodically by the group to identify weaknesses and make any necessary changes.

Instructions

1. Begin by reading the essay "Effective Group Skills" (see below) as an outside class assignment prior to the in-class exercise of completing the checklist and answering the discussion questions on the worksheet.

2. Working individually, place a check beside those norms that all members of your group have been following.

3. Compare your answers with others in your group, and discuss ways of improving your group's effectiveness and your experiences with others in the group.

Grading

Instructors can choose to grade this assignment and your participation in this exercise in a variety of ways. Check with your instructor for grading details for your class. First, it is very important that you know and understand what distinguishes effective groups from ineffective groups. Specifically, what are the core activities of effective groups? Instructors can include questions such as these on an examination. In addition, instructors who emphasize an active learning approach in their classrooms frequently include class participation as part of a student's grade for the course. Most important, you should know that this exercise has implications for how well both you and classroom groups perform and how well you actively learn the concepts and theories of sociology.

Reading: Effective Group Skills

This class and book are designed to involve you as a group member in the fundamental concerns of sociology. It is important that you understand the conceptual and empirical knowledge of sociology addressed here. Equally important, from an active learning perspective, is to gain a practical understanding of this knowledge through the group structure of this classroom. Everyone is a member of groups outside class, and this social fact will apply to your involvement in this class. Your participation in your classroom group should contribute to your understanding of social interaction and the application of sociological knowledge to other everyday life situations outside the classroom. Yet for this to be successful it is important that you understand what is expected of you as a group member if you and your groups are to be effective.

As individuals we have all experienced memberships in a variety of groups in society. Obviously some of these group experiences have been more important and significant for us than others. Furthermore, if we reflect on our different group experiences, we will recognize that some group experiences have been quite positive and productive, while other group experiences have been negative, unproductive, and maybe even a waste of our time. What distinguishes effective groups from ineffective groups, and what interpersonal skills are necessary for constructing and maintaining positive, productive, and effective groups (both here in the classroom and in our daily lives)?

To be a member of an effective group you will need to understand how your behaviors and the behaviors of others contribute to the overall success of your group. Social scientific studies of small groups have determined that an effective group is are characterized by the following three core activities: (1) accomplishing group goals or objectives; (2) maintaining itself internally; and (3) developing and changing in ways that improve its effectiveness. Each of these core activities will be briefly discussed.

Before a group is able to accomplish its goals, the group must first clearly articulate and understand what its goals are. It is therefore important that you understand the instructions and objectives of group activities before your group begins any activity. Briefly review any rules or directions and discuss these with other group members. Most important, each person in the group should have a high degree of commitment to accomplishing these goals.

Groups maintain themselves internally when each individual's identity is related to his or her group. Group cohesion (or togetherness) should be high. As much as possible, group members should be accepted, included, supported, and trusted. Members must be willing to communicate their thoughts and feelings freely and openly and must be open to the thoughts and feelings of others in the group. Conflict and controversy should be viewed as inevitable and as essential components of group life; members should respect the beliefs of others, even when different from their own. Finally, all members of the group should come to class and be there on time, and they should participate and be fully involved in group activities and discussion. And, whenever possible, all members should take turns assuming leadership responsibilities.

Groups must also be willing to evaluate themselves and to change their behaviors and ways of doing things when necessary. There should be a continuous process of changing and devising new strategies to meet different situations. If the instructor provides feedback or suggestions about your group, you should reflect on ways that you might modify or change your behaviors.

Last, each group should remember that they are part of a larger group—
the entire class. The classroom is organized in such a way that groups can
view other groups, and some group activities might actually involve different
groups interacting with other groups in the classroom. Just as there are different groups in society, so too are there different types of groups that make
up this class. This classroom, like society, can be viewed as a collection of
individuals and groups, all of which are in interaction with one another.

At the conclusion of each group activity the instructor will want each
group member to focus his or her attention on the larger class group. It is not
only important that you experience the various group activities, but you must
also make sense of what the activity was all about sociologically. Why did we
do the activity? What did you think about, and how did you feel while doing
the activity? What are the implications of the activity to you, to our groups,
and to our society? What sociological concepts or social processes are illus-
trated by the group activity? The class will address these and many other
questions. Be sure to focus your attention and contribute your insights to this
larger class discussion.

Initial Group Assessment

Effective Group Skills Worksheet

Name: _____

(Students should make copies of this form for future use in the course)

Checklist:

_____ All members arrive on time and attend all class sessions.

_____ No one dominates group discussion and all members actively participate in group exercises.

_____ All members share thoughts, ideas, and feelings freely and honestly.

_____ Everyone listens to what others have to say without interrupting them.

_____ Conflicts and disagreements are viewed as natural and are handled productively.

_____ Leadership responsibilities are shared and/or people take turns being the leader.

_____ Members of this group respect each other and recognize individual differences.

_____ The overall "atmosphere" of the group is relaxed, informal, and comfortable.

Discussion Questions:

1. According to this checklist, what are the strengths and weaknesses of your group?

2. How has your group changed in ways that make the group more effective and productive? Are there any new weaknesses or strengths?

Panel Debates

Kathleen R. Johnson, Keene State College

It is better to debate a question without settling it than to settle a question without debating it.[1]

Rationale

Today's complex social and environmental problems challenge our basic understandings of the world, and solutions to these problems call for critical-thinking and problem-solving skills. This assignment requires each student to organize and conduct a small group or team debate during class. Upon its completion, I hope you will be more knowledgeable about a particular social issue and more skilled in making arguments to support your own claims and beliefs. This assignment also provides an opportunity for you to become more involved in the class and to work collaboratively with others on a project that includes public speaking and open debate.

Instructions

Early in the semester, you will be randomly assigned to a panel composed of three students and a specific date for your debate. Your group will then be randomly assigned a broad social topic (e.g., gender, crime, families, or race). From this broad topic your group must select a key question that will provide the focus for your panel debate. For example, on the general topic of crime, you might consider and debate one of the following questions: Is gun control an effective means of reducing crime? Should getting high be illegal? Should we continue to privatize the prison system? Is capital punishment justified?

Specific steps to follow:

> Step 1: Determine the viewpoint (for/against/neutral) that each person will take in the debate. Two of your group members will take a stand on the issue (for/against) and the third will serve as an issue-neutral moderator and media-event analyst. (I describe these roles in more detail below.)

Step 2: Individually prepare for your contribution to the debate. Each member should have equal time to present his or her position to make various points and to summarize his or her perspective.

Step 3: Schedule a meeting to rehearse the debate. This meeting will help you become familiar with each person's role and position on the issue.

Moderator Role: The moderator prepares nameplates and introduces the panelists and the issue that they will debate. The class will need to know the general dimensions of the problem: Who is concerned about or affected by it? As a way to introduce the issue, the moderator (after consultation with the group) will choose an issue-related media article for analysis and class presentation. For example, your group may agree to debate the pros and cons related to genetic cloning or the effects of an aspect of welfare reform. You should be able to find an interesting (usually controversial) article from the media on either of those topics. Your contribution to the debate should incorporate (a) a summary of the article, (b) an analysis of how your selected article depicts the social problem, and (c) a brief review of the history of the social problem that your group is studying. In general, the moderator frames the debate by providing background material. Use the media material to assist you.

Panelist Role: It is not sufficient that either panelist merely asserts his or her position. Try to present your view on the basis of evidence and good reasons. To help you with forming your position on your topic, you might want to consider the sociological perspectives discussed in this course as a way of organizing your thoughts, establishing criteria on which to base your reasoned opinions, and determining what evidence to present. You can use overheads, videos, handouts, or other visual aids in order to make your perspective as effective and as interesting as possible. We can all agree that the position you take on the issue does not necessarily reflect your personal views on the matter. It is important to remember that the degree to which we understand any opposing viewpoint directly relates to the level of confidence we can justifiably have in our own convictions.

Audience Role: Everyone plays a role in making this activity an engaging class experience. Listen attentively; show respect for the speakers. Take part in the discussion or planned activity. Students can ask the panelists questions at any time. Anyone (including the panel members) can challenge another on matters such as the definition of terms; unstated value premises; the lack or misuse of evidence; reliance on authorities whose expertise was questionable; the pertinence, reliability, and validity of evidence; and the adequacy of logic.

Grading

Check with your instructor for details on grading this exercise. Generally, the following questions will be considered when evaluating the moderator: How effective was the overview of the issue or problem presented by the moderator? Did the media analysis touch upon some of the key points related to the issue? Did the moderator ask the panelists follow-up questions and call on people in the class who wanted to ask questions? The evaluations of the two panelists are based on the following questions: How effective was their initial presentation of the problem from their perspectives? How well did they defend their positions? (That is, how consistent were they in remaining in their roles as proponents or opponents?) Did they use any educational tools during the course of the debate?

In general, the evaluations will be based on the following criteria: (1) substance or content (reflected in the position on the issue), (2) creativity and resourcefulness (use of materials or exercises), and (3) form and style (articulation, length, organization, and preparedness). In determining your final grade for this assignment, your instructor may take into consideration the evaluation of your peers using the anonymous evaluation form.

Note

1. Joseph Joubert, quoted in "Learning from Debate," by Lawrence Carter-Long. *Animals' Agenda,* July/August 1997, Vol. 17, No. 4, page 28.

Panel Debate

Evaluation Form and Worksheet

Evaluation: This evaluation is a confidential group evaluation. Please rate yourself and your peers on the following criteria (0 = lowest score, 5 = highest score).

1. List the name of each panelist in the first column. Be sure to include your name and evaluation as well.

2. To what extent did each member of the group attend the meetings in preparation for the debate?

3. To what extent did each member fulfill the obligations, if any, of the meetings that you held in preparation for the debate?

4. Did each member participate in a positive manner with other group members?

5. Did each member participate in class with all responsibilities fulfilled?

6. How would you rate the overall contribution of each member?

1. Name	2. Attendance	3. Obligations	4. Participation (Group)	5. Participation (Class)	6. Contributions Overall

Your Reaction to the Assignment: What general things did you learn from this assignment? Do you have any suggestions for improving this assignment? (Use back of worksheet, if needed.)

About the Editors

Kathleen McKinney received her Ph.D. in sociology from the University of Wisconsin–Madison in 1982 and is professor of sociology and the Cross Endowed Chair in the Scholarship of Teaching and Learning (SoTL) at Illinois State University (ISU). From 1996 to 2002, she held the administrative position of Director of the Center for the Advancement of Teaching at ISU. McKinney is a social psychologist with interests in relationships, sexuality, sexual harassment, higher education, and college teaching. McKinney has numerous scholarly publications, including several books and dozens of refereed articles in these areas. McKinney is involved in the SoTL movement at the national and international levels, working with the Carnegie Academy for the Scholarship of Teaching and Learning (CASTL) Campus Program and as a founding member of the International Society for the Scholarship of Teaching and Learning (IS-SoTL). She frequently gives workshops on SoTL to faculty at other institutions and has written *Enhancing Learning Through SoTL* (2007). Last year she received Fulbright Senior Specialist Candidate status for possible foreign travel to engage in faculty development work. She served three years as editor of *Teaching Sociology* and sits on various SoTL journal editorial boards. McKinney is also a member of the American Sociological Association (ASA) Department Resources Group, a group of about 60 sociologists who conduct teaching workshops and program reviews and write/edit teaching materials. She is also active in the ASA Section on Teaching and Learning in Sociology. McKinney was a 2003–2004 Carnegie Scholar and has received several teaching awards, including ISU's College of Arts and Sciences Junior and Senior Distinguished Teacher and Outstanding University Teacher, the ASA Hans Mauksch award for contributions to undergraduate education, and the ASA Distinguished Contributions to Teaching Award.

Barbara S. Heyl received her Ph.D. in sociology from the University of Illinois at Urbana-Champaign in 1975 and is professor emerita of sociology at Illinois State University. For thirty years at Illinois State University she taught sociology at both the undergraduate and graduate levels, specializing in the sociology of deviant behavior and qualitative research methods. During this time she served four years as graduate coordinator of the Sociology Master's Program and one year as interim director of the School of Social Work. She also served as secretary and as president of the Midwest Sociological Society. Her most recent research involved a longitudinal, qualitative study of special education in Germany supported by Fulbright and the Deutscher Akademischer Austausch Dienst (German Academic Exchange Service) awards, with results published both in Spain and the United Kingdom. Her past research on prostitution led to a classic book based on life history and ethnographic interviewing (*The Madam as Entrepreneur,* 1979). She has published articles on the positive effects of using collaborative methods for both teaching in the college classroom and for conducting field work for research purposes, including a chapter on ethnographic interviewing in the *Handbook of Ethnography* (Sage, 2001). Co-presenting with William Rau and other colleagues, she has had extensive experience conducting workshops on collaborative learning and other active learning techniques (20 in the U.S. and 5 in Thailand), all at the post-secondary level. She was awarded Outstanding Teacher of the College of Arts and Sciences, 2001, and University Outstanding Teacher, 2003, at Illinois State University. Heyl was recently granted Fulbright Senior Specialist status to support faculty development efforts overseas. She is currently active in local Peace and Green movements.